A FINE PLACE FOR A CITY
Titus Bronson and the founding of Kalamazoo

by

NICK KEKIC

Kalamazoo   1984

Cover: 1834 plat map of Bronson Village.
Courtesy, Western Michigan University,
Waldo Library Map Department.

Copyright 1984   All Rights Reserved
ISBN 0-9613850-0-6

   Publisher
Nick Kekic
Oak Opening Press
P.O. Box 811
Kalamazoo, Michigan 49005
   Printer
Fine Books Division
Taylor Publishing Company
   Dallas, Texas

CONTENTS

Dedication

For my Kazoo School history students who were
there at the beginning:

Athena Malloy	*Tony Clark-Lee*
Beth Allgood	*David Newbury*
Dawn Peters	*Kim Balcolm*
Jay Klosterman	*John Ford*
Jon Harrison	*Morgan Gaughn*

Special thanks to Linda Newbury, who was there at
the end.

Acknowledgments

Many people contributed to the editorial process which produced this book. My sincerest thanks to: Robin Nott, Debbi Ochala, Rick Hulsey, Linda Newbury, Susan Williams, Judy Ranger, Bill McCall, Jerry Brown, Norma Malloy, John Cooley, Martin Grossman, Marcia Meyers, William Grimshaw, Ruth Moerdyk, and Nancy Nott.

In their own unique ways Sonita Newbury, Richard Anderson, Jon Weeldreyer, Curtiss Clark, David Snelling, Mary Lubelski, Phyllis Burnham, Arlene Shub, John Stites, Catherine Larson, and Chris Morgan contributed significantly to the creation of this book. To them I express my deepest appreciation.

A Note on Documentation

This book was researched and written over a period of almost six years. Unfortunately, some bibliographic information was lost in the process. Notwithstanding this defect, I have chosen to include the undocumented material because it plays an essential role in the story of Titus Bronson and the founding of Kalamazoo.

Titus Bronson, the founder of Kalamazoo. Notice the potato on the table. Original oil painting by pioneer artist Benjamin Cooley, 1870. Courtesy, Kalamazoo Public Library.

Preface

We all have our own Walden Ponds; places of retreat where we seek peace and perspective to counter the complexity of everyday existence. One refuge of mine is the Local History Room in the Kalamazoo Public Library. There, during the fall of 1978, I began researching the life and times of Titus Bronson, the founder of Kalamazoo.

I had begun studying Kalamazoo history with a group of children at the Kazoo School, an independent elementary and middle school then located in the Vine Neighborhood. Because Titus Bronson's name was so prominent in our community — Bronson Park, Bronson Boulevard, Bronson Methodist Hospital — our first research assignment was to find out all we could about him: who he was, where he came from, and what he did.

I went to the Local History room fully expecting to find a biography of so significant a historical figure as the founder of Kalamazoo. When I didn't find one, I was curious and puzzled. I examined Willis Dunbar's history of Kalamazoo. He observed that, "Sometimes it seems that the people of Kalamazoo are just a bit ashamed of the founder of their city, his eccentricities, his sloppy clothes, and his queer habits."

Dunbar was right. One evening while waiting on a customer at a local bookstore, I encountered an excellent example of what he meant. A woman in her mid-twenties paid for some books by check. Her last name was Bronson. "Do you know anything about your family history?" I asked. She shook her head back and forth. The smile disappeared from her face, replaced by a frown. She replied, "No, and I don't want to know because I might be related to that weird guy."

In the Michigan Pioneer Collections I discovered a biographical sketch of Titus Bronson written by the 19th century Michigan historian A.D.P. Van Buren, who related this summary of Bronson's character given by someone who knew the founder personally:

He was eccentric in many things, but a man of noble impulses, generous to a fault, as long as he had anything to give; scrupulously honest and upright himself, he could have no patience with dishonesty or meanness in any form. Strictly temperate, he was particularly bitter and outspoken in his denunciation of those who drank liquor or used tobacco in any form. His denunciation of politicians as a class was by no means flattering to them, as he took no pains to conceal his disgust at their dishonesty and sharp practice; and I have the impression that this had not a little to do with the exchange of the name from "Bronson" to "Kalamazoo."

He was a fast talker, and he knew a great deal about many things. He had read many books, had a good memory, and in talking, gave his opinions without stint, and maintained them without fear, or flinching. He was slovenly in the general adjustment of his dress, and general appearance. Although he pretended to shave, his face usually showed like stubble land at harvest time. He wore his coat as he did his mittens, only when it was necessary, but usually went without either. He walked by fits and starts; would sometimes stop suddenly, take off his coat, and start on the run; and ere he had gone far would stop and put on his coat again.

Titus Bronson was a natural frontiersman. He belonged to the advanced Leatherstocking grade of civilization, and loved the ways of frontier life better than town life.[1]

After reading this description something happened inside me. The necessity to learn everything I could about the founder of Kalamazoo took hold. A few weeks later I decided to write a book about Titus Bronson. In July, 1979, I hitchhiked to Tallmadge, Ohio and Middlebury, Connecticut. Titus was born and buried in Middlebury. He lived in Tallmadge, now a suburb of Akron, before emigrating to the Michigan Territory. In both these states I discovered significant sources of information about the life and times of Titus Bronson.

Questions are the engines of the intellect. They help transform curiosity into controlled inquiry. I commenced my quest for the historical Titus Bronson by asking myself a series of questions: Why was he so restless? Why did he move around so much: from Connecticut to Ohio to Michigan to Illinois to Iowa? Why was he never satisfied with one particular place? To answer these questions it was necessary for me to go back and study the basics of American history with an eye for information and insights that would help me understand the life and times of Titus Bronson.

There is a dearth of information about the founder of Kalamazoo. This book is a collection of five intradependent essays that tie together the knowledge we presently have about Titus Bronson. Each chapter covers different territory in an attempt to answer certain questions, such as: What did Kalamazoo look like as a wilderness? Who lived here before Titus Bronson arrived? Why was Kalamazoo chosen as the county seat? What was the world view of Titus Bronson? What religion did he profess? What were his politics? How did his Puritan family roots influence him? Was Titus Bronson a Yankee in the classic American sense? Why was he so eccentric? Was Titus Bronson a frontiersman? Was Titus Bronson a tragic hero?

My particular vantage point as a historian is based on the premise that if you understand something about Titus Bronson and the inner workings of his character in the context of the times in which he lived, you might increase your understanding of contemporary American history, and perhaps of yourself.

Nick Kekic
Summer, 1984
Kalamazoo, Michigan

Notes

[1] A.D.P. Van Buren, "Titus Bronson, The Founder of Kalamazoo," in *Michigan Pioneer Collection,* vol. 5, 2nd ed. (Lansing, Michigan: Robert Smith Printing Company, 1900) pp. 369-370.

Bronson Park Indian Mound, 1984. Photograph, Linda Newbury.

CHAPTER ONE:
OAK OPENING WILDERNESS TO COUNTY SEAT

An elderly Potawatomi Indian stood on South Street in downtown Kalamazoo, facing Bronson Park. It was the 1870's. She had returned to visit the place of her birth. Sad-eyed and silent, she looked westward, feeling lost. She scanned the park looking for something familiar, a landmark to remind her of those long-ago days of her childhood. Her eyes focused on a grassy knoll in the southwestern corner of the park and she exclaimed:

O, I know where I am now for there is the mound on which I used to play when I was a girl. That used to be our attractive playground. There, long years ago, I used to meet with many other children of our people and on top of that mound, and on its green side, we spent many happy days.[1]

Chances are that the origin of the Bronson Park mound goes back to the time of Christ, when a group of prehistoric cultures known as the Hopewell flourished over a vast area of the eastern North American continent, including Kalamazoo County. When Titus Bronson arrived at the present-day site of downtown Kalamazoo sometime during the summer of 1829, he found not only the mysterious mound but also one of the most curious of all North American

5

antiquities, the so-called "garden beds" — low ridges of soil approximately 18 inches high, arranged in a variety of geometrical patterns which resembled formal gardens. Except for a few reported in Indiana and Wisconsin, these garden beds were unique to Michigan. The ten acre plain south of the Bronson Park mound was covered with garden beds in the shape of wheels with spokes. Samuel Durant, in his 1880 history of Kalamazoo County, wondered if the beds could "have been some excessive plats where flowers were raised for the supply of some great city on Lake Michigan or in the Ohio Valley?"

During the summer of 1832, two Kalamazoo pioneers, E. Lakin Brown and Cyrus Lovell, dug up the innards of the Bronson Park mound. Brown described the dig in a letter he wrote:

> . . . We began an excavation near the top of the mound, and sunk it to near, or quite to a level with the surrounding plain — perhaps not quite. We discovered nothing whatever — no bones, no pottery, no implements, or relics of any kind. A little charcoal was all. The earth removed, was a dark soil, apparently the surface soil of the adjacent plain.[2]

Titus Bronson may have spent his first night sleeping on ground near the Bronson Park mound. Like the ancient ones who came before him, Titus Bronson also had dreams and plans — to found a great city named after himself that in 20 years would have railroad service to Detroit and the new country further west. "Here is a fine place for a city," Bronson told himself, "Here I will pitch my tent and spend my days. This is the Canaan of which long I've dreamed. This will be the county seat."

One common misconception of the American frontier maintains that the frontier was a trackless wilderness covered by primeval forest. The example of the Kalamazoo County frontier wilderness offers a refutation of this falsehood. The travels of generations of Indians had hewn out primitive highways. Native Americans made so many paths and trails that it would have been possible to travel from coast to coast, although no one, as far as we know, ever did. Potawatomi Indians crossed Kalamazoo County with a series of trails that in many cases predated modern highways. West Michigan Avenue (formerly Main Street) in downtown Kalamazoo was once part of the great Washtenaw Indian trail. Westnedge Avenue, Oakland Drive, Gull Road, and Douglas Avenue — all were well-worn trails.

Kalamazoo County as a wilderness offered three types of habitable landscapes to the pioneers: heavy beech-maple forest, prairie land, and oak openings. In 1825 a pioneer who laid out a farm on the Huron River in Washtenaw County wrote that "the interior of Michigan is delightful — a mixture of prairies, oak openings and woodland, abounding in clear streams, fine lakes and cold springs .. . a rolling country well-adapted to good roads." The same could have been said about the wilderness landscape of Kalamazoo County. The oak openings were a landscape that lay along the borderland where woodland met prairie. In this wilderness borderland, the pioneer encountered the best of both worlds — wilderness with the charm of a finely-cultivated garden.

Surveyors who transformed the Michigan wilderness into real estate frequently used the word "barrens" to designate an oak opening landscape. In the 1820's the emigrants from New England and New York brought with them the term oak openings — meaning a landscape of scattered oaks — usually white oaks — with little under-growth except grass. Oak openings were usually undulating and hilly. The rare burr oak opening was a special type of oak opening that was usually level and covered with burr oak trees. The burr oak opening or burr oak plain was considered more valuable than an ordinary oak opening because the former's soil was especially fertile.

There were two burr oak plains in Kalamazoo County, one on the present site of downtown Kalamazoo. In 1831 Henry Little arrived in Kalamazoo. Later he wrote:

At that time there were no fences nor roads, nor any well-defined paths. This whole plain was carpeted with a bright green grass, much resembling an old meadow. There were no small shrubs, nor underbrush. Small burr-oak trees, here and there, dotted the landscape, giving it

7

something of the appearance of an old apple orchard; had the burr-oaks been in regular rows, the resemblance would have been more perfect . . . The Kalamazoo mound was situated nearly in the center of this plain which contained several hundred acres. We can but admire the correct judgement of the Mound builders, for their selection of this beautiful and inviting place, on which to erect this wonder-inspiring memorial of their genius, of their industry, and cultivated skill.[3]

A year later another Kalamazoo pioneer, Jesse Turner, came to Kalamazoo. His description of the wilderness site of present-day downtown differs significantly from Henry Little's. Turner reminisces:

There is quite an idea that this village site was a grassy plain with scattering burr oaks; but it was a plain covered with thick and tall hazel brush, so thick that I have seen a wolf jump up so as to see what caused the row he heard; and the burr oaks were very small, little more than grubs . . . There was perhaps an acre of clear ground about the mound in the park, and a few rods south of the jail was always a mud hole that I used to think was where the dirt was carried to make the mound.[4]

The discrepancy in descriptions was due to the rapid changes that occurred to the oak openings when the settlers arrived. The annual fall fires set by the Indians to keep away the underbrush stopped. A vigorous growth of young timber began. John Muir, founder of the Sierra Club, grew up in the oak opening wilderness of Wisconsin. Muir in his memoirs, explained what happened when the fires stopped:

As soon as the oak openings were settled, and the farmers had prevented running grass fires, the grubs (roots) grew up into trees, and formed tall thickets so dense that it was difficult to walk through them, and every trace of the sunny oak openings disappeared.[5]

As the landscape changed so did the way of life for the predominant Indian nation in Kalamazoo County, the Potawatomi, a word meaning "people of the place of fire."

By the 1820's when the white settlers started to trickle into Kalamazoo County, the Potawatomis' way of life had been influenced by European civilization. French and English fur traders had been operating in the area for almost a quarter of a century. The Indians became dependent on the material goods and physical trappings of white culture. They had discarded their deerskin hunting shirts and dresses for garments of brightly colored calico. They used blankets instead of buffalo robe or bearskin. They were dependent on the traders for many of the necessities of life; they purchased much of the same hardware and dry goods as the white settlers.

According to Bronson family history, Titus Bronson was on friendly terms with the Potawatomis and some authorities say that they helped him build his claim shanty out of tamarack logs cut along the banks of Arcadia Creek. His eldest child, Eliza, used to tell this story:

> An Indian chief, who frequently came to my father's house, one day asked my mother if he could take me — I was six or eight years old — home with him to his wigwam. My mother, fearing to offend the Chief by refusing his request, allowed him to take me away with him. After being gone all day, the Chief brought his little charge back to her home just at twilight but how different I looked. I was most gaily and fantastically decked off with feathers and ribbons of bright colors, and other Indian finery.[6]

Titus Bronson arrived in the Michigan Territory in the spring of 1823. He purchased a couple of parcels of land in Ypsilanti Township, in Washtenaw County. In the summer he landed jobs working in a sawmill and on a farm in Oakland County. After spending the winter with a family with the surname Williams, Titus Bronson moved to Washtenaw County in the spring of 1824. John Geddes, an early settler of Ann Arbor, and an acquaintance of Bronson's, wrote in a letter, "The first time I saw him [Bronson] was the 13th day of July 1824; he was working in his potatoes in a place then called Snow's landing, now called Rawsonville, four miles below Woodruff's Grove, on the Huron." In the fall of 1824 Bronson made a deal with John Allen, one of the co-founders of Ann Arbor; Bronson traded land he owned near Ann Arbor for another parcel in nearby Pittsfield Township. Geddes tells us: "On this quarter-section there was a handsome plain; Titus got some boot; I don't know how much; I heard him say not enough."

Another early Ann Arbor pioneer, Henry Osterhout, remembered Bronson arriving in Ann Arbor with a wagon, three yoke of oxen, and a wooden plow.

> *He was the first man who brought potatoes to Ann Arbor — you could not get them from Detroit or anywhere . . . Titus broke up a quantity of land potatoes, and although he had eighty bushels of potatoes you could not buy of him; he was going to plant them and make money out of them. He had made his money in Ohio planting potatoes. While hunting up a place he stayed at our house and furnished potatoes for his keeping. My mother took the eyes out of the potatoes and we planted them — the first of anybody in Ann Arbor.[7]*

Titus Bronson made his living for many years as an itinerant potato farmer. His nickname on the Ohio and Michigan frontiers was "Potato Bronson." The money he used to purchase his Kalamazoo County lands was made from a potato crop raised in Washtenaw County. As the story goes, a Mr. Gilkey of Indiana, who lived in a log cabin on a stream called Neshannock, introduced Bronson to the practice of potato farming. Mr. Gilkey showed Bronson a variety of potatoes named after his home stream. Titus was impressed by what he saw and purchased a batch of Neshannock potato balls. Titus's first crop yielded a high price: thus began his career as a potato farmer. He would travel from one neighborhood to another, growing them and then selling his product. Bronson village gained a reputation early in its history as a place where one could purchase good potatoes. Potatoes grown by Titus Bronson were the first product of what is today Kalamazoo.

Records of Titus Bronson's travels from 1825 to 1829 are vague. He spent much of his time traveling in Ohio and Michigan searching for the ideal place for his county seat. Founding a county seat was one of the most ambitious, prestigious and lucrative goals an entrepreneur could achieve during the first half of the nineteenth century. City building was a risky do-it-yourself activity that required much nurturing, planning and perseverance.

In January, 1827, at the age of 38, Titus Bronson married a widow, Sally Richardson, in his hometown of Middlebury, Connecticut.

In the spring of 1827 the newlyweds moved to Tallmadge, Ohio. There they started a family — a daughter, Eliza was born to them. In Bronson village, Sally Bronson gave birth to two children, a son who died in infancy, and another daughter, Julia. Both of the Bronson daughters married men from Illinois and lived their adult lives in that state.

From the time of Jamestown and Plymouth until the end of the nineteenth century, land-hungry husbands uprooted their families to head west through forest, prairie, and mountain pass. Historians are finally beginning to research and write about the role of pioneer women in the westward movement. Pioneer men like Titus Bronson had the opportunity to range over the wilderness, enjoying the richness of the wildlife and scenery. Pioneer women like Sally Bronson had to toil indoors, often in a crude cabin bereft of windows, deprived not only of friends and neighbors, but even of the simple joy of looking at the sunlight and enjoying the seasons. Pioneer women, at times, lived hideously hard lives. Their husbands, whose stories have dominated the history of the westward movement, were very dependent on their wives for emotional and physical support. "I never do anything without consulting her," Hector St. John de Crevecoeur wrote of his wife in *Letters from an American Farmer* (1782). The same was true of Titus Bronson. It was his wife who possessed the good business sense and acumen. When Titus went to the land office in Monroe to purchase his Kalamazoo County lands he put the deeds in his wife's name. When asked on what terms he would sell certain lots, Titus would respond in his typical eccentric and repetitive way, "Ask her, ask her."

Jesse Turner, who was a friend of both Sally and Titus Bronson, described Sally as "a smartish sort of woman" who was "a little inclined to dictate. One day when she had been more than usually vigorous, Titus handed her his pantaloons, jerking out the words, 'Take'em, take 'em.'"

Titus Bronson often talked on and on, describing his dreams and plans for his settlement's future. One time a cynic in Bronson village told the founder "that in twenty years the tired and hungry traveler wandering this way would not be able to find a solitary hut in Bronson." On hearing this negative prediction, Titus Bronson grew indignant, and responded vigorously, that "in twenty years from this time you will see a large city here and you will be able to go to and from Detroit in one day by the railroad cars."

And yet, one night in the fall of 1830, Bronson was ready to give up his rights to his townsite claim for $100 and a gun to one of his neighbors from Ann Arbor, Samuel Camp. Camp and his friend Sidney Ketchum spent that fall trekking through the prairies and oak openings of southwestern Michigan, looking for land to buy and speculate with. Camp and Ketchum traveled to Titus Bronson's claim on the Arcadia Creek and were impressed with what they saw. Throughout the evening, as they sat around a campfire in the chilly October night air, Ketchum attempted to persuade Bronson to sell his rights for $100 and a gun. Titus finally gave in to Ketchum's pressure and agreed to the deal. The next morning, while Sally was preparing breakfast for the company, Titus told her that he had sold their rights to the townsite claim. Sally was furious, telling Titus that he had no right to go and sell their land without consulting her. Then she asked her husband, "Whose name is on that deed?" Titus didn't have a response, and at breakfast he told a disappointed Ketchum that the deal was off.

A new settlement and its surrounding hinterland were wedded together. The key question the Bronsons asked themselves was: What services will our city supply which will attract an urban population to purchase town lots? That's where the money was.

On the Michigan frontier the urban services most desired by the agricultural population were gristmills, sawmills, retail facilities, and governmental services, making a settlement suitable for the county seat designation. The political, economic, and social focus of the county would be the seat of government. Michigan's territorial governor, Lewis Cass, understood this fact. In 1817 he issued a policy dealing with the selection of county seats. As Cass saw it, the location of the county seat should be a compromise between its geographical center and the distribution of its population. Another factor was "compensation from the person who will be benefited by this location." Compensation could take the form of town lots, money, labor, or materials for the public buildings.

Titus Bronson's first step towards making his dream of founding a county seat in the Michigan wilderness come true was to become a sqautter and establish a pre-emptive claim on a suitable site. He finally decided on the southwest quarter of section 15 in Kalamazoo Township. This 160 acre tract is now bounded by Patterson Street on the north, Westnedge Avenue on the west, Lovell Street on the south, and, roughly, the Kalamazoo River on the east. Bronson built a claim shanty near the present-day intersection of Kalamazoo and Westnedge Avenues. He roofed the tamarack log cabin with grasses from the banks of Arcadia Creek and built a crude fence around the cabin. As the weather started turning cold, he headed south along what is today Westnedge Avenue to Prairie Ronde, where he spent the winter with Basil Harrison and his family.

Basil Harrison was a patriarchal figure who died at the fabulous age of 103. A native of Maryland, Harrison's uncle (Benjamin Harrison) signed the Declaration of Independence. Basil Harrison's cousin (William Henry Harrison), the famous leader of the 1811 Battle of Tippecanoe, would become president in 1840, and the latter's grandson (Benjamin) would follow him in that office in 1888. While a boy, Basil Harrison emigrated to Pennsylvania with his family. As a young man, he headed west and settled in Clark County, Ohio. At nearly sixty years of age, Basil Harrison began feeling restless. His brother returned from a trip to Michigan with a glowing report of the fertile soils and valuable timberlands in the Michigan Territory. Impressed by the account of his enthusiastic brother, Harrison sold his holdings in Ohio and set out for the Michigan Territory in September, 1828, leading a party of twenty-one people. They followed roads as far as Fort Wayne, Indiana. However, the trek northward took place on well-worn Indian trails. After a month of traveling and bushwhacking, the party emerged from the woods and stood on the southeastern border of Prairie Ronde, the largest of eight prairies in Kalamazoo County. The Harrison party spent their first night on the edge of Prairie Ronde. The next day they were greeted by Chief Sag-e-maw and a group of Indians. Basil Harrison communicated to them their desire to settle near water. The Indians guided the pioneers to a small lake three miles northwest of the present village of Schoolcraft. There, Basil Harrison built his home and lived out the rest of his life. He died in 1874, and at his funeral, over a thousand people gathered in the village of Schoolcraft to pay tribute to the person considered to be the first permanent white settler of Kalamazoo County.

If you happen to be flying over Kalamazoo County on a clear day, take a look below and you will see a vast checkerboard consisting of fields, roads, and cities laid out in a precise north-south, east-west arrangement. The only features which don't run by the compass are the prairies, valleys, rivers, ridges, and streams. The system of land survey underlying this checkerboard scene was conceived in large part by Thomas Jefferson and promulgated in the Land Ordinance of 1785. Under the provisions of this ordinance the vast public domain was to be divided into townships six miles square, by lines running due north, south, east, and west. The townships were then divided into 36 separate square-mile sections of 640 acres each. Over two million square miles have been divided into townships. There are over 1200 townships in Michigan. Essentially the same system of surveying is still used in Alaska today.

Under the leadership of Lewis Cass, a New Hampshire native, Michigan adopted the New England model of local government, called the "town" in New England and the "township" in Michigan. Cass and the Territorial Council believed strongly in local self-government. The first step, usually, was for the Council to "establish" a county. This entailed giving a county a name and specific location. Then it was temporarily attached to an adjacent organized county. When the population grew to a certain point, another act was passed "organizing" the county, giving it the right of self-government under the laws of the territory. Kalamazoo County was established in October, 1829. It was attached temporarily to St. Joseph County. The next month, November, 1829, the Territorial Council ordered that all of Kalamazoo County, along with Barry County and the country north as far as the Grand River, should constitute the township of Brady.

It should be noted that there were "survey" townships and governmental units like Brady, also called townships. Generally, governmental townships corresponded with the survey townships, although during the first few years of Kalamazoo County's existence, governmental townships such as Brady included numerous survey townships. In July 1830, when Kalamazoo County was officially "organized," Brady township shrank in size to include only the southern half of Kalamazoo County. The northern half was to constitute the governmental township of Arcadia, which included the survey townships of Cooper, Richland, Ross, Oshtemo, Comstock, Charleston, and Kalamazoo. According to the 1830 organizational act, the first Arcadia township meeting was to "be holden [sic] at the house of Titus Brownson [sic]."

No records exist of that historic first meeting which was held in April, 1831. However, a year later, on April 3, 1832, the first recorded election took place in Kalamazoo County at the home of Titus Bronson. Caleb Eldred was chosen supervisor of Arcadia Township. Titus Bronson was elected as one of the "Overseers of the poor" and one of the "Pound-masters."

In the spring of 1830 Titus Bronson headed south to Tallmadge, Ohio where his wife Sally and their daughter Eliza had spent the winter. During the summer the Bronson family, along with Sally's brother Stephen Richardson, traveled in a covered wagon pulled by oxen to their new home in the wilderness of Kalamazoo County.

During the spring of 1830, while Titus Bronson was in Ohio gathering his family together, a federal pre-emption law was passed stating:

> If two or more persons be settled upon the same quarter section, the same may be divided between the two first actual settlers . . . and in such case the said settlers shall each be entitled to a pre-emption of eighty acres of land else where in said land district.[8]

Titus Bronson manipulated this "floating claim" provision — the eighty acre claims were called floating claims and were often sold — to his advantage. When he and Stephen Richardson journeyed to the Monroe federal land office to file and pay for Bronson's pre-emption claims in Kalamazoo and Prairie Ronde, Titus Bronson asserted that Richardson had also occupied and cultivated lands on Bronson's first pre-emption claim and thus had a right to the land on Prairie Ronde. The Kalamazoo County tract book records that on November 1, 1830, Bronson purchased the east half and Richardson the west half of the southwest quarter section 15, in Kalamazoo Township. At the same time they each purchased half of the northeast section 14, in Prairie Ronde Township. This strategy was obviously illegal, but one used frequently by speculators who wanted to speculate in two desirable locations with one claim.

Although Titus Bronson was the first settler, the noteworthy distinction of building the first house in what is today Kalamazoo belongs to William Harris. In the spring of 1830, Harris, who was also Bronson village's first black settler, built a "shed-roof" log cabin for his wife and three children on a site where Westnedge and Water Streets intersect. A shed-roof log cabin was composed of poles slanted in one direction covered with marsh grass. The cabin had an earth floor. In cold or damp weather blankets and shawls were hung against the windows and doors.

Another arrival during the spring of 1830 was Nathan Harrison, one of the many children of the county's first settler, Basil Harrison. The young Harrison built a log cabin close to the confluence of the Kalamazoo River and Portage Creek, and established a ferry service there. He operated a large scow for teams and a canoe for travelers on foot. Historian Samuel Durant wrote that Harrison "was wont to enjoy himself catching fish while his spouse managed the ferry business." In 1835 the first bridge was built across the Kalamazoo River. The bridge put Harrison and his wife out of business, so they emigrated to Illinois. According to Durant, Harrison

> belonged to that class of men who Col. Daniel Boone and Cooper's 'Pathfinder' were illustrious examples — men who, when the clearing around their cabins became so extensive that they could not fell a tree within ten rods of it, abandoned the country and sought a region where they were not likely to be crowded by neighbors.[9]

In January 1831 Titus Bronson met with commissioners appointed by Territorial Governor Lewis Cass at the site of his pre-emption claim in Kalamazoo Township. Titus's site was one of three considered by the commissioners as a possible county seat. Some settlers of Prairie Ronde thought the county seat should be "on the Portage stream, near the geographical center of the county." But no settler had pre-empted such a location and therefore no person was present to bargain for the consideration of this specific site. Consequently, the commissioners decided that the advantages of such a site, "although of some magnitude, were not considered to take the site from the benefits to be derived from the navigation of the [Kalamazoo] River."

In addition to the Prairie Ronde site and Bronson's in Kalamazoo Township, the waterpower site where Comstock Creek entered the Kalamazoo River received some consideration by the commissioners. The commissioners wrote in their report, "Two places upon the river, about the same distance from the center of the county, presented their claims for the site. These were examined with care and not without anxiety." But the claims of the creek were not argued very forcibly because the only building there was a shack erected by Caleb Eldred, who was back east at the time, gathering his family for a final move. Although settlers from Toland's Prairie met the commissioners at the creek, no land owners were present to bargain for the county seat designation like Titus Bronson did for his site.

The commissioners wrote in their report to Lewis Cass:

A spot was at length selected on an eminence near the center of the south-west quarter section fifteen, town two, south, of range eleven, west owned by Titus Bronson, Esq. Mr. Bronson has agreed to lay out a village, and place upon the proper records a plan or map thereof, duly acknowledged, with the following pieces of land, properly marked and set apart in said map or plan for public use: One square of sixteen rods for a Jail; one square of sixteen rods for an academy; one square of eight rods for Common Schools; one square of two acres for a public burial ground; four squares, of eight rods each, for the four first religious denominations that become incorporated in said village, agreeable to the statute of the Territory.

This place is situated at the great bend of the Kalamazoo River, on the southwestern bank, immediately below the Portage stream. The reasons which influenced the location of the county seat at this place are: 1st. It is on the bank of the river, which at that place is navigable, most of the year, for keel boats of several tons burthen, 2nd. It is in the direct line between the two largest prairies in the county, viz: Prairie Ronde and Gull Prairie; about nine miles from the latter, and about ten miles from the former place, and Grand Prairie two miles on its west. 3d. Good roads may with facility be made from it into any part of the county. Four or five large trails set out from this place, leading to as many places of importance on the St. Joseph and Grand Rivers. 4th. The great Territorial road passes through it.

Your Excellency is therefore respectfully recommended to establish, permanently, the county seat at the place above mentioned.[10]

This report was submitted by the commissioners on January 15, 1831 and approved by Lewis Cass on April 12, 1831. As historian Samuel Durant commented, "From this time dates the beginning of a long and prosperous career for one of the finest villages in the land."

True to his promise to the commissioners, during the spring of 1831 Titus Bronson traveled to the Monroe land office and registered the first plot of the village, which he named after himself. It included the land from Westnedge to Portage, and from South Street to North Street. Separate squares were designated for the courthouse, jail, and school. Also, the first four churches to organize and request building lots would receive land. As a result, numerous churches stand today adjacent to Bronson Park. Titus Bronson and Stephen Richardson were the sole proprietors of this first plat. Titus hired Phinias Hunt, a mathematician, to draw up the plat. As Kalamazoo historian Peter Schmitt has pointed out, Hunt's problems as a surveyor can still be observed in the Vine neighborhood south of downtown where Westnedge jogs at Lovell Street. At this location Hunt designated the corner of the original plat several feet west of the proper section line.

News of the county seat designation and the platting of the village soon spread far and wide. The population of the village increased rapidly. Some of the permanent settlers who arrived in 1831 were Dr. Jonathan Abbott, the first doctor and postmaster of Bronson village; David S. Dillie, the first brick manufacturer, came from Gull Prairie and built a log cabin near the old Central High School in the present-day Vine neighborhood; Hosea B. Huston built the first store on the northeast corner of West Michigan and Rose Streets; Cyrus Lovell, the first lawyer, arrived from Vermont. Titus Bronson and Nathan Harrison kept open house for the new arrivals until they could build their own homes with the help of Elisha Hall, the village's first carpenter.

In the fall of 1831 General Justus Burdick arrived in Bronson village. A friend of Burdick's who later became the first attorney general of Michigan, Elon Farnsworth, advised Burdick to go West because it would be to his financial advantage. Burdick took his friend's advice and came to Detroit, where he met Lucius Lyon. Lyon told Burdick about Bronson village's designation as the county seat and advised Burdick to buy land there. As a result, Burdick purchased, from Titus Bronson, the east half of the southwest quarter of section 15, with the exception of four lots Bronson had sold to others. The land cost $850 and the deed was executed in Detroit at Elon Farnsworth's office. After the transaction Justus Burdick returned to Vermont and sent his brother Cyren Burdick to look after his interests in Bronson.

1832 saw more new settlers and investors arrive in Bronson village. During this year Justus Burdick's future business partners, Lucius Lyon and Thomas C. Sheldon, became owners of land in and around the village. In the spring of 1832 Cyren Burdick, backed by his brother's capital, began construction of the village's first regular hotel and tavern, the Kalamazoo House, which was located at the intersection of Michigan and Portage Streets.

The previous winter Titus Bronson had built a sawmill on Portage Creek. He employed Rodney Seymour to operate the mill. Soon after, Cyren Burdick purchased the mill from Bronson and instructed Seymour to produce most of the lumber used in construction of the Kalamazoo House. The building was a two-story frame structure with a two-story veranda along its front. It was opened to the public in September, 1832. Three years later, the Kalamazoo House and lot were taxed to Justus Burdick, Lucius Lyon, and Thomas C. Sheldon at a value of $2,000. The same year, 1835, Johnson Patrick opened a formidable rival to the Kalamazoo House on the northwest corner of Michigan and Rose Streets, the Exchange Hotel.

The first death in Bronson village occurred at the Kalamazoo House soon after it opened; the name of the person is lost to history. The year 1833 opened with the village's first marriage, between Ethan French and Matilda Hounsom. The ceremony was performed by Cyrus Lovell. By the spring of 1833 there were about fifteen settler families and 100 people. In addition were the Potawatomi Indians, who were still quite numerous in the area. The Indians brought fish and game to the settlement, where they were exchanged for money and goods at Hosea Huston's store. Village lots were selling at prices ranging from one dollar to fifty dollars. Supposedly Justus Burdick offered a new arrival a partnership in his unsold village property at $5 per acre. This apparently good deal was declined. Among the new settlers in 1833 were Ira Burdick, a brother of Justus and Cyren, who became the keeper of the Kalamazoo House; Abraham Cahill, who established the first tannery; and Daniel Cahill, who opened a furniture store.

Lewis Cass's decision to designate Titus Bronson's Kalamazoo Township site as the county seat did not end competition for the county seat designation. About the same time Cass made his decision, a wealthy lawyer from Cooperstown, New York, Horace C. Comstock, arrived in Kalamazoo County with the same ambition as possessed Titus Bronson — to found a county seat whose name would immortalize his family surname.

Horace Comstock was married to the niece of novelist James Fenimore Cooper, a distinction which gave him instant status among his peers and acquaintances in the Michigan Territory. Comstock was a popular person. He was a skilled and subtle promoter and politician, smooth, suave, charming, handsome, and witty — basically everything Titus Bronson wasn't.

Henry Little was a pioneer who knew most of Kalamazoo County's earliest settlers, including Titus Bronson and Horace Comstock. This is how Little viewed the competition for the county seat designation:

But of all places on this earthly ball, the Creek was to be his [Comstock's] darling, favorite pet, the object of his special fostering care, and place of abode. Nothing was to be feared from the pretended rivalship of that half-crazy, eccentric Bronson, way down there by the river. Bronson's place was geographically wrong; it was low and wet, and would be unhealthy; and besides all that, Bronson was entirely alone and without money, and friends and influence. But Comstock had the right location, and money, and friends, and influence, and would have the county seat.[11]

Horace Comstock was also a wheeler-dealer type who made a great deal of money in the Detroit-Chicago trade of military supplies, domestic articles for Indians, and trader materials. Comstock arrived in Kalamazoo with about $5000 in cash and a strong ambition to increase his wealth, power, and status through land speculation. At the June, 1831 land sale and in the following year, Comstock purchased about 1700 acres of government land. By 1836 it was reported that his worth reached $500,000. In 1835 he persuaded his wife's uncle, James Fenimore Cooper, to invest $6000 in western lands, assuring the author of a large profit. Six months later, Cooper changed his mind and asked for his money back. Comstock didn't have the cash so he gave Cooper four notes, due at different times, representing the sum invested plus $2500 profit and $150 interest. Comstock paid the first two notes when they fell due, but defaulted on the other two. However, Comstock redeemed the fourth note by transferring to Cooper the titles to eighteen lots in the village of Bronson. Twelve of these lots now form the block bounded by Burdick, Kalamazoo Avenue, Edwards, and Willard Streets. The other six lots were south of Kalamazoo Avenue between Burdick and Edwards. Cooper held these lots until his death in 1851. (His will is part of the probate records of Kalamazoo County).

Horace Comstock's attack on the established county seat in Bronson was based on three arguments. Comstock contended that his village was as close to the geographical center of the county as was Bronson village. He also argued that his settlement had waterpower facilities superior to those at the established county seat. To prove his point, Comstock offered as evidence the gristmill and the two sawmills operating in his village. Lastly, Comstock argued that Comstock, not Bronson, was the true head of navigation on the Kalamazoo River.

In 1832, Horace Comstock built a warehouse and landing on the Kalamazoo River at his village and erected a storehouse for the protection of goods that were to be shipped to and from the village at the mouth of the river.

During the fall of 1832 settlers from various parts of Kalamazoo County met at Bronson village to decide on the question of the county seat. The meeting didn't have any legal standing but nonetheless was a democratically significant event, giving the citizens a chance to speak out on the critical issue. Although details of the meeting are unknown, it might have been conducted as a formal debate, with Titus Bronson and Horace Comstock arguing their respective cases before their neighbors and friends. It may have been one of Bronson's greatest moments.

Let your imagination go and picture a hat being passed collecting the ballots of the pioneer settlers packing the log cabin. The tension in the air is thick with expectation and the unknown. Titus Bronson fusses and whittles while Horace Comstock sits, cool and calm. The results are announced and Titus Bronson breathes a big sigh of relief. His village has won the vote and his dream of founding a county seat in the oak opening wilderness of the Michigan Territory was still intact.

But Horace Comstock didn't give up his hopes. In 1833 he erected a schoolhouse at his own expense, simply asking that in return the citizens should call the village and township "Comstock," a name that had already become quite popular. The same year he opened a store at the village. Comstock enjoyed a decent trade with the settlers of the surrounding country, who added to the hustle and bustle of the village by their frequent calls for lumber, store supplies, and grain grinding. Comstock and his wife also built a fine residence with handsome grounds. Their home gave the village an air of refinement and culture that left a pleasant impression of the whole place upon the beholder. A traveler who passed through Comstock in late 1833 described the village:

> I passed the previous night at the little hamlet of Comstock, where an enterprising young gentleman, after whom the place is called, having the advantage of a good mill-seat, is creating a flourishing establishment around him; a frame-store and several log cabins, with two or three mills, already giving some importance to the situation in a new country.[12]

Finally admitting defeat for the county seat designation, in 1837 Horace Comstock purchased a quarter interest in the village plat of Kalamazoo for $17,000 and in 1844 he moved to Kalamazoo.

Notes

[1] Alexis A. Praus, "The Kalamazoo Mound: A Letter from Alexander J. Sheldon." *Michigan History,* December, 1960, p. 392.

[2] ibid., p. 392.

[3] ibid., p. 386.

[4] Jesse Turner, "Reminiscences of Kalamazoo," in *Michigan Pioneer Collection,* vol, 18, 2nd ed. (Lansing, Michigan: Robert Smith Printing Company, 1900) p. 582.

[5] Aldo Leopold. *A Sand County Almanac* (New York: Ballantine Books, 1970) p. 32.

[6] A.D.P. Van Buren, "Titus Bronson, The Founder of Kalamazoo," in *Michigan Pioneer Collection,* vol. 5, 2nd ed. (Lansing, Michigan: Robert Smith Printing Company, 1900) pp. 370-371.

[7] Henry Osterhout, "Five Minute Speeches of the Pioneers Present," in *Michigan Pioneer Collection,* vol. 18, 2nd ed. (Lansing, Michigan: Robert Smith Printing Company, 1900) p. 19.

[8] Bernard C. Peters, "Early American Impressions of the Landscape of Inner Michigan with Emphasis on Kalamazoo County" (Master's Thesis, Michigan State University, 1969) p. 198.

[9] Samuel W. Durant, *History of Kalamazoo* (Philadelphia: Everts and Abbott, 1880) p. 219.

[10] Peters, p. 203.

[11] Durant, p. 389.

[12] Charles F. Hoffman, "Michigan as Seen by an Early Traveler," *Michigan History,* May 1925, p. 431.

Early Bronson village courtroom scene. Titus Bronson is the judge sitting at the table on the far left. Courtesy, Kalamazoo Public Library.

CHAPTER TWO:
A MAN OF NOBLE IMPUSLES

When we said that he was tall and spare and sun burnt, with a countenance bespeaking intellect and determination, we described a man as he appeared to us . . . Few men possessed a memory so tenacious of whatever came within its grasp. Reading was to him a source of infinite pleasure, and whatever he read, he treasured up, apparently without effort, and could be referred to years afterwards with reliability.

Thus spoke Frederick W. Curtenius about the founder of Kalamazoo on a beautiful summer day in June 1854. A crowd of 300 people gathered together in what is today Bronson Park to celebrate Kalamazoo's 25th birthday. The formal program, organized by the Ladies Library Association, was held at Kalamazoo County's first courthouse, a white frame building on the north side of Bronson Park where the present court building now stands. The celebration concluded with a feast at Fireman's Hall, a building that stood where John W. Rollins, Bookseller is located on today's Kalamazoo Mall. After the delicious and sumptuous meal, over forty toasts were offered to the village and its people. Judge Webster offered a toast to "the memory of Titus Bronson, one of our earliest pioneers, and the first proprietor of a part of the plat of Kalamazoo." The Reverend Menkzie offered a toast to the man who had given the main address at the Bronson Park ceremonies earlier in the day. "To Colonel Curtenius, the farmer, the citizen, and the orator."[1]

When he was 29 years old, Frederick Curtenius emigrated to Kalamazoo County from New York. He later became a Civil War hero for defying his commanding officer's order to return some slaves to their owners. Frederick Curtenius knew Titus Bronson well. He often encountered Bronson on roads, in fields, or in the forest. Curtenius told his Bronson Park audience that in such encounters, Titus Bronson would sometimes "run over the history of Rome, Greece, and Carthage, from the day they were founded to the day they crumbled." Of Bronson's mind and manner, Curtenius stated:

> [Bronson's] mind was a store-house of historical facts, strangely mingled with chimeras. The world was not created exactly in accordance with his ideas of propriety and perfection; nor was society formed precisely upon the right basis. His study seemed to be, to devise plans for rectifying both . . . Eccentricity, coupled with an abrupt and unfortunate freedom of speech, reckless of his audience, begat in the minds of many a bitter dislike for him.[2]

"Eccentric" is the most frequent adjective used to describe Titus Bronson. One pioneer friend of Bronson's commented that he "was eccentric in many things, but a man of noble impulses, generous to a fault, as long as he had anything to give." It seems that two distinct Titus Bronsons emerge from descriptions of him. On the one hand, he is portrayed as a kind and generous person who often helped people. On the other hand, he was bitterly disliked by many of his neighbors.

Why was Titus Bronson so eccentric? Why did some of his neighbors dislike him so much? The answers to these questions may be rooted in the interplay between Bronson's spiritual life and his nervous system. Titus Bronson supposedly walked by fits and starts. He would stop suddenly, take off his coat, start off on the run, stop again, put on his coat, and then begin running. It is entirely possible that Titus Bronson possessed some type of nervous disorder which contributed to his eccentric behavior.

About thirty years after Bronson's death in 1853, a French doctor, Georges Gilles de la Tourette, first described what is today known as Tourette's Syndrome, a neurological disorder that afflicts over 100,000 Americans, and four times as many men as women. This syndrome is a nerve disorder that manifests itself as a form of tic or habit system where the sufferers lose control over speech and movement. Bronson's behavior in the courtroom during his lawsuit with Marcus Hounsom may be a manifestation of Tourette's Syndrome.

Titus Bronson and Marcus B. Hounsom entered into a partnership together in 1832 — Hounsom constructed a sawmill on Portage Creek, and Bronson acted as his partner. Eventually Hounsom sued Bronson. The suit was tried before Jesse Turner and Samuel Percival. Cyrus Lovell was Titus Bronson's lawyer. During the trial Titus became nervous and fidgety, as was normally the case when he was in trouble. At such tension-filled moments, forgetting what he was about, Titus would whittle a cane, a book, or anything he could get hold of with his jackknife. On this particular occasion, Bronson could not find anything to whittle, so he went to the window and began to cut the sash. Seeing this odd behavior, Cyrus Lovell cried out in the middle of his argument before the judges, "Bronson! What are you doing there? Don't cut that window; you are the damnedest man I ever saw." Bronson, in an excited and dazed manner, retorted, "Well, well, I don't know what I am about; this matter perplexes me so. I would rather have the life lease of a Frenchman than this pesky sawmill."

Titus Bronson's nervous eccentricity often carried over into the courtroom. He was the type of person who, at times, believed in taking the law into his own hands. During his years in Bronson village (1829-36) he was constantly embroiled in legal controversy. For example, in April, 1833, Joseph Eddington chopped down a cherry tree on unclaimed land "with the intention of using the same to make furniture," according to the court record. But Titus Bronson "seized the tree and carried away the same without the consent of the plaintiff, knowing at the time that the plaintiff had cut the same."[3]

The dispute was brought before Judge Basil Harrison. The next month a jury of six people decided that Bronson was guilty and fined him the cost of the tree — $4.62 ½ — plus the court costs of $10.25. Titus appealed the case to circuit court, but to no avail.

Titus Bronson was also a justice of the peace and often found himself personally in the middle of the case at hand. Once in a matter before the circuit court, Titus Bronson's docket as justice of the peace was brought in as evidence. Judge Fletcher, looking at the docket, said "it was more like anything else than a justice docket." At this, Titus reached out, seized the record, opened the stove door, and threw it into the fire, exclaiming, "Well, well, if I can't keep a docket, I can raise potatoes."

In 1835 the circuit court ruled that Bronson had misused his post as justice of the peace by seizing two cattle belonging to a Brady Township settler. This seizure went back to another incident four years earlier. At that time, Bronson, as justice of the peace, levied a judgment against a man named Harry Smith who was accused of trespassing by Elisha Hall. Smith never paid his judgment, which steamed Titus, who, two years later went to Smith's homestead and "with force of arms . . . seized, took, and drove a certain yoke of cattle . . . of great value to wit of the sum of $60."

Harry Smith retaliated by bringing a trespass suit against Titus Bronson. The trial was held in May, 1833. Bronson contended that he had a right to do what he did because he was justice of the peace. His peers on the jury ruled against him. Titus was fined $60 plus court costs of $7.71. But the frontier legal battle continued beyond that. The bitterness between Harry Smith and Elisha Hall continued to fester. Smith contended that in the original 1831 suit Bronson had ruled wrongly against him. Smith then decided his next step would be to sue Hall and call Bronson as his key witness. When Hall's lawyer called the founder to the witness stand, Bronson, without "consent or pronouncement" left the courtroom, apparently quite upset. The court record read that Bronson had "gone to somewhere to this plaintiff unknown and could not be found." Without Bronson as a witness, Smith was forced to drop the suit.

William James in his groundbreaking *Varieties of Religious Experience* (1902) contended that a religious and spiritual life intensely pursued often produced exceptional but eccentric people. Such persons, he wrote:

> . . . *are geniuses in the religious line, and like many other geniuses who have brought forth fruits effective enough for commemoration in the pages of biography, such religious geniuses have often shown symptoms of nervous instability.*

William James labeled people who behave in an eccentric and intense manner, like Titus Bronson, as "cranky." Some characteristics of the cranky state of mind include:

— *extraordinary emotional susceptibility.*
— *liability to fixed ideas and obsessions.*
— *a tendency for conceptions to pass immediately into belief and action.*
— *a refusal to rest when possessed by a new idea until it is proclaimed or in some way worked off.*

"What must I do about it?" as opposed to "What shall I think of it?" is the cranky mind's usual response to a problem. Cranky "true believer" types of people do not remain mere critics and intellectuals, argued James, but, "Their ideas possess them, they inflict them, for better or worse, upon their companions or their age."

Ideas possessed the mind of Titus Bronson. His tendency to inflict those ideas on his neighbors was what "begat in the minds of many a bitter dislike for him." Bronson manifested in his behavior the world view of a true believer. A true believer is a person who combines enthusiasm and knowledge with frustration and fear in order to create a world view that provokes a passionate intensity and a proclivity for action. Titus Bronson possessed the temperament of a true believer. This, combined with his nervous disorder, made him an exceptional and eccentric man and also accounted for his restlessness and social isolation.

Undoubtedly, Titus Bronson was an exceptional and eccentric person. He pursued his religious and spiritual life with a passionate intensity. He was "a friend to the religion of the Bible," a true Christian believer and perfectionist whose values went back to the founding of America by the Puritan emigrants from England in the 17th century. The Bible commanded, "Be ye therefore perfect as even your Father which is in heaven is perfect." This passage is the basis for the doctrine of perfectionism — the notion that people could become sanctified while living on earth. The very term Puritan was coined to describe the desire for perfection, and the idea of perfectionism has been a constant theme in American history. As Alexis de Tocqueville wrote in *Democracy in America:*

> *Americans have a lively faith in human perfectability. The idea of perfection, of a continuous and endless amelioration of social conditions, this idea is presented to the American unceasingly, in all its aspects.*

Titus Bronson's religious affiliations in Bronson village are unclear. It is frequently asserted that he was one of the twelve founding members of the First Methodist Church, but apparently no documentation exists to support this assertion. The first formal sermon preached in Kalamazoo by a minister of any denomination took place in 1832 at Bronson's house. The preacher was a Methodist circuit rider named James T. Robe. Cyrus Lovell once said that Bronson "kept everybody that came to his house, especially the ministers." One example of this involved a young seminary student. In the fall of 1831 the Rev. O.C. Thompson, fresh from Princeton Theological Seminary, traveled to the Michigan Territory bearing a commission from a national benevolent society. Thompson's description upon encountering Gull Prairie for the first time is noteworthy:

> *That afternoon my eyes were gladdened by the first sight of a prairie in its native wilderness. The sky was clear and sun just setting as I emerged from a thick forest and came all at once upon the Gull Prairie; a gentle breeze was swaying the tall*

grass to and fro, and the scene was more than beautiful, it was sublime.

Eventually, the young missionary made his way to the frontier settlement of Bronson. He arrived at Titus Bronson's house — which he called "a house of entertainment" — just as a Baptist minister was leaving. The departing preacher, Thompson related, "bowed to the landlord, who, by the way, was called a pretty hard man, and said, 'Mr. Bronson, I wish you would treat my Master as well as you have treated me.'" Thompson continues, stating that Bronson treated him in the same generous manner.

Historian Peter Schmitt summed up Titus Bronson's character as follows:

His name was Titus Bronson, and people in Michigan remembered him. Some called him a drunkard, others said he never drank. Some thought he was tall and others short. But however vague their recollection, most found Kalamazoo's first settler a comic figure. In the language of the time he 'was slovenly in the general adjustment of his dress.' He looked thin and nervous, walked 'by fits and starts,' talked entirely too rapidly, and repeated himself over and over. He argued every question and had no time for shrewd dealing. His face, said one pioneer, looked 'like stubble land at harvest time' when he shaved. Another said that 'he ran with his lame leg as no other man could run; he laughed as no other man could laugh; he te-heed, and showed his long teeth, stretching his mouth from ear to ear, as no other man could.' The best that could be said with certainty about him was that he was eccentric, read a great deal, shared what he had with his neighbors, and hoped for better times.[4]

Overall, this paragraph is an accurate description of Titus Bronson, with two exceptions. By the authority of Frederick Curtenius's description of Titus Bronson as "tall, spare, and sun burnt" we can say with certainty that he had a tall and lanky physique. The other point concerns Bronson's drinking habits. Titus Bronson, unquestionably, did not drink, and yet to this day, many people believe that he was run out of Kalamazoo because he was a drunkard.

Several stories illustrate the degree of Bronson's dislike for intoxicating drinks. For example, one day he was dining with an old friend. Titus loved pickles and ate very heartily of the pickles on the table. He asked his friend's wife how she made such excellent pickles. She replied, "I put the cucumbers into so much water, so much whiskey, and let them remain so long before using them." Titus jumped from the table and exclaimed, "Woman, woman, I've been eating horrible poison." Titus thrusted his finger down his throat and then ran out of the house to rid himself of those poisonous pickles.

Hosea B. Houston built a still on the shores of the Kalamazoo River in a secret location he named "Clip-knockie." Houston then built a boat to travel up and down the Kalamazoo River, peddling his product. He painted the boat's name on its side with red paint: "Titus Bronson of Clipknockie."

E. Lakin Brown was an early Kalamazoo County pioneer who knew Titus Bronson well. In a letter Brown wrote he shared the following information which reveals Titus Bronson's true believer personality.

Titus Bronson was at Kalamazoo when I arrived there in the fall of 1831, and I took my first meal at his house. He passed the winter of 1830-31 at Prairie Ronde; that is about the first I heard of him. He was a very eccentric man, and had his hobbies, one of which was his passion for Neshannock potatoes, which he introduced into the country, and which he raised in great quantities — hence his soubriquet of 'Potato Bronson.'

He was an exceeding thin, spare, man, very dark, with a perpetual grin; had a quick, abrupt way of talking, often repeating a word or phrase two or three times in succession. When applied to for terms on which he would sell certain village lots, his reply was: 'Ask her, ask her,' meaning Sally, his wife.

The last time I saw him was at Stephenson, Illinois, where, in 1837, he was keeping hotel.

*While we were at dinner he mentioned the recent
death of a former prominent citizen of Schoolcraft at Dubuque. Quite shocked, I asked of what
disease he died. 'Rum fever — rum fever — rum
fever,' he said, so rapidly you could scarcely
distinguish the words. He had a great hatred of
rum and all its evils, and my impression is that he
was a man of strict integrity, of strong prejudices,
and perhaps bigotry. He was altogether comical
in appearance and manner. He would start and
run on any little occasion, cutting a most funny
figure with his long, lank legs, dark, grinning
face, twinkling black eyes. That's about all I know
of him.*[5]

Another aspect of Titus Bronson's life that can be dis-
cussed with some certainty is his political stance. A few
months preceding his arrival in Kalamazoo County the
summer of 1829, Andrew Jackson was inaugurated as the
seventh president of the United States. From the Declaration of Independence in 1776 to Jackson's inauguration in
March, 1829, the country grew from thirteen colonies to 24
states. In the election of 1828, Jackson defeated John
Quincy Adams in the popular vote. Jackson won the
electoral college 178 to 83. Adams carried New England
and parts of the central Atlantic region. Jackson made a
clean sweep of rural hinterland west of New Jersey and
south of the Potomac. One Adams backer said, "A great
revolution has taken place." Another wrote, "It was a howl
of a raving democracy." Many Americans saw Jackson as a
direct political heir of the American Revolution. As one
editor wrote during the 1828 campaign, Jackson would
"bring back the republic to the purity and simplicity of the
democratic days of the country."

The 1830's saw the birth of modern party politics in
America. The two dominant parties were the Jacksonian
Democrats and the Whigs. Deep value conflicts were
embedded in the party cleavages. To comprehend the
Whig-Democrat clash it is useful to look at their values on
an authoritarian-laissez faire spectrum. On issues relating
to government regulation of ethics, morals, and beliefs, the
Whigs tended to favor control while the Democrats

resisted it. The Democrats believed in the traditional liberalism which emphasized the separation of law and morality. The Whigs favored a government which would demand compliance to specific community norms and mores from its citizens. The Whigs also wanted a paternalistic national government acting to promote economic development. The Democrats wanted fewer restraints on the individual and tended to reject the Whigs' integrative approach, whether in morals, religion, culture, or national political economy. Ralph Waldo Emerson, who contended that "Morality is the object of government," came to disapprove of the Democrats — he labeled them the "rank-rabble party" — because "they did not base political action on morality, or shape their politics toward the promotion of individual culture."

The Whigs saw themselves as the party of decency and respectability, guardians of piety, sober living, proper manners, thrift, steady habits, and book learning. The Democrats, for many, were by definition hard-drinking, dissolute, and hard-living folk, or at least sympathetic to such behavior. Protestant Democrats tended to belong to nonevangelical denominations. This evangelical vs. anti-evangelical conflict can be placed in the perspective of a dispute at least as old as the republic. Beginning in the 1790's activisit Protestants attempted to reclaim America for the deity. After the War of 1812 national benevolent societies proliferated, hoping to put a Bible in every home, promote missions, preserve the Sabbath, support Sunday schools, save the Indians, extirpate demon rum, wage peace, revive backsliders, and much more. The Yankee Whigs, as they settled the frontier, carried a righteous and confident urge to use the secular government to create a morally perfect and unified society.

What were Titus Bronson's political views? How did he feel about the election of Andrew Jackson? Where did this eccentric Connecticut Yankee frontiersman fit on the political spectrum of Jacksonian America? We know that he did not like politicians as a class of people, as historian A.D.P. Van Buren tells us: "His denunciation of politicians as a class was by no means flattering to them, as he took no pains to conceal his disgust at their dishonesty and sharp practice."

On October 2, 1835, the following letter to the editor appeared in Bronson village's weekly newspaper *The Michigan Statesman*. The letter provides evidence that Titus Bronson was a "Federalist," a term often used during this era of American history to describe persons opposed to Andrew Jackson and the policies of the Democratic Party.

Messrs. Editors: It has been frequently asserted, recently, by C. Lovell, esq. and his federal supporters that he is friendly to the President [Jackson] and his administration. Now I have been acquainted with Mr. L's politics for three years past and I know that on all occasions, until about the time he came out as a candidate for the legislature, denounced the president and his measures, and I have been informed, by many persons who knew him well before he came to this country that he was always violent in opposition to Gen. Jackson.

It is pretended, too, that he is friendly to Mr. Lyon. How are these facts? Mr. Lovell was the loudest and longest in denouncing the nomination of Mr. Lyon last spring, spoke of him as a man of feeble talents, and was a member of a committee, who drew up and reported resolutions pointed directly against Mr. Lyon, in a meeting called for the avowed purpose of defeating his election. These facts are capable of judicial proof.

A man is best known by the company he keeps. Mr. Lovell's political friends and associates are the bitterest federalists in this county.

By whom was he nominated for Representative? Was there a single democrat present at his nomination? I put the question directly and it must be answered in the negative.

The truth is he received his nomination from Jim Smith, D.E. Brown, and H.G. Wells in connexion [sic] with that Prince of disorganizers, Daniel G. Garnsey. I say nothing against Mr. Lovell, but I sincerely believe he has no love for the demo-

*cratic party or its principles, for surely, if he was
attached to either, he would not suffer himself to
be made use of by federalists to defeat the wishes
of those to whom he professes to be friendly. Can
it be seriously credited by anyone, that such
people as J. Smith, jr., Doct. Brown, Titus Bronson,
Anthony Colley and Steven Vickery would aid in
the election to any office, a man whom they
supposed to be friendly to democracy? It is impos-
sible. Still these are the very men on whom Mr.
Lovell relies for these things.
One who despises double faced politicians
Toland's Prairie, Sept. 28, 1835[6]
(emphasis added by author)*

A week after this letter appeared, voters in Kalamazoo
County and the rest of the Michigan Territory overwhelm-
ingly approved the proposed state constitution. Election of
state officials also took place at this time, and the Demo-
crats carried the county, as they did the rest of the
Territory. Cyren Burdick was elected to the state house.
Horace Comstock was elected to the state senate. Lucius
Lyon was elected as Michigan's first United States senator.
All three of these men were staunch Democrats.

Undoubtedly, one of the chief reasons Titus Bronson
was so unpopular with many of his Bronson village
neighbors was his outspokenness on political issues. As
historian A.D.P. Van Buren has written, Titus Bronson

*was born and bred in the land of steady habits,
and his love of truth, temperance, honest dealing
between man and man, virtue in both public and
private life, was ingrained in his mental and
moral growth, and you might as well have under-
taken to move Plymouth Rock by the force of
denunciation and threats, as to make Titus Bronson vary one hair's breadth from his high moral
standpoint, or palliate vice or wrong in the public
or private act of any man. He was determined to
hew to the line, let the chips fly as they would.
Coming in contact with men and their opposition, sharpened instead of smoothed the angles of
the man.[7]*

During the second quarter of the 19th century, a tremendous surge of true believer reforming energy, enthusiasm, and ambition transformed the lives of thousands of Americans. A common phrase of the time was "a sisterhood of reforms," an umbrella concept which one contemporary described as "a variety of social and physiological theories of which one was expected to accept, all, if any." Antislavery, temperance, women's rights, health reform, school reform, communitarianism — all these movements greatly benefited from the momentum created by the Protestant perfectionist evangelical awakening of the 1820's and 1830's, which inspired thousands of Americans to social activisim. Perfectionism could be egocentric with little social content. But it could just as easily become an energizing principle, providing inspiration to people who wanted to manifest moral integrity in all aspects of their everyday lives. The majority of these perfectionists-turned-reformers were evangelical Protestants of diverse persuasion and occupation from New England families. Their strength was greatest in New England and its cultural provinces such as the Western Reserve of Ohio, where Titus Bronson emigrated in the early 1820's.

In 1840 Ralph Waldo Emerson attended a convention of social reformers to listen to their dreams and visions for establishing the perfect society and world. The gathering took place on Chardon Street in Boston, and was organized by the Friends of Universal Reform. Emerson wrote in his journal that among those present were:

> Madmen, mad-women, men with beards, Dunkers, Muggletonians, Groaners, Agrarians, Seventh-Day Baptists, Quakers, Abolitionists, Calvinists, Unitarians, and Philosophers — all came successively to the top, and seized their moment, if not their hour, wherein to chide, or pray, or protest.

What impressed Emerson the most — even more that the tremendous variety of garb and speech and the overall eccentricity of the participants — was their "prophetic dignity" amid opposition and ridicule. However, Emerson didn't trust moralism as a motivator for human beings. He was skeptical of social reformers because he was skeptical of the true believer state of mind, fueled by the powers of discontent. Nonetheless there is much truth to the saying that "Discontent is the mother of progress." Discontent and the quest for personal and social perfection are the two sides of the coin of restlessness that has been the currency of social reform in the United States throughout its history.

We must be careful not to throw out the baby of enthusiasm with the bathwater of fanaticism. The word enthusiasm is derived from Greek roots meaning "possessed by god." Enthusiastic true believers of passionate intensity, are indeed possessed of a spirit that enables them to go further than their contemporaries. The great explorers and discoverers have been enthusiastic true believers, typified by Columbus who would not let himself be persuaded by those who assured him, with a wealth of scientific evidence, that if he sailed to the edge of the world he would fall off. Paralyzing fear of enthusiasm is as dangerous as its fanatical excesses. Enthusiasm and its achievements start with feeling, not with reason. Rejection of enthusiasm is rejection of feeling, a deadly path for the human species.

The history of social change is the history of enthusiastic true believers in action. *Dreamers of the American Dream,* (1957), by Stewart Holbrook describes such Americans, of which Titus Bronson is a prototype. Holbrook believed that an individual can have an immense effect in influencing the forces that make history. He concluded his book by paying homage to the motley collection of dreamers and visionaries he wrote about:

> *I choose to think, or perhaps only I feel, that the United States today is infinitely 'a more perfect union' than that conceived by the Founding Fathers. By 'union' I do not mean only our political arrangements. I mean a more perfect society. For all its many faults, it is a society in which life, liberty, and the pursuit of happiness are recognized as never before to be the rights of all. These rights were not ours simply because of a bold statement in the Declaration. We got them, in large part, during the past one hundred and eighty years, by the efforts of assorted dreamers*

and visionaries who were basically seeking perfection . . . They dreamed nobly, and they acted. Taken all together, they were enormously effective in making the United States a better place to live than it otherwise would have been and is. They were a daft, earnest, honest, and all-but-incredible lot of men and women. I think of them as sort of a national conscience.

The same is true of Titus Bronson. The founder of Kalamazoo can be viewed as a sort of local conscience whose life — although flawed with an aura of fanaticism — is one worthy of study and emulation. Thanks to Titus Bronson's noble vision of human perfection, Kalamazoo has a tradition of social conscience rooted in its beginnings as a city.

Notes

[1]"Address of Col. Curtenius," *Quarter Centennial Celebration of Kalamazoo, Michigan* (Kalamazoo, Michigan, 1855), pp. 12-26.

[2]Ibid., p. 17.

[3]Barbara Walters, "Bronson's Odd Behavior Contributed to His Legal Woes," *Kalamazoo Gazette,* September 11, 1983.

[4]Peter J. Schmitt, *Kalamazoo — The Place Behind the Products* (Woodland Hills, CA: Windsor Publications, 1981), p. 17.

[5]A.D.P. Van Buren, "Titus Bronson, the Founder of Kalamazoo," in *Michigan Pioneer Collection* Vol. 5, 2nd ed. (Lansing, Michigan: Robert Smith Printing Company, 1900), p. 370.

[6]*Michigan Statesman,* October 2, 1835.

[7]Van Buren, p. 368.

Author Nick Kekic at Titus Bronson's gravesite in Middlebury, Connecticut. The epitaph reads: "A western pioneer returned to sleep with his fathers." Photograph, Curtiss Clark.

CHAPTER THREE:
The Puritan Roots of Titus Bronson

Off Route 64 in Middlebury, Connecticut, nestled amongst rolling hills and meadows, a half-mile from the village green, is the cemetery where Titus Bronson was buried over 130 years ago. (He died at his brother Leonard Bronson's Middlebury home on January 6, 1853). The epitaph inscribed in his thin old gravestone reads, "A Western Pioneer Returned to Sleep With His Fathers." Nearby, to the north, Breakneck Hill borders the horizon. Middlebury lore tells us that in the late 17th century a team of oxen broke into a tiff while climbing Breakneck Hill. One gored the other, and the victim stumbled, fell, and broke its neck. Thus the name Breakneck Hill, where the founder of Kalamazoo was born on November 27, 1788.

Twice during the Revolutionary War, General Rochambeau and 4,000 troops encamped at Breakneck Hill. June, 1781 found them on their famous march to Yorktown, Virginia, where the Revolution was won with Washington's defeat of Cornwallis and the British. In October, 1782, on their return trip, the victorious troops once again encamped at Breakneck Hill. During both camping expeditions it rained, making conditions cold, muddy, and wet. It is no surprise General Rochambeau accepted Josiah Bronson's (Titus Bronsons' great-uncle) invitation to spend the night at his home, a quarter-mile from the encampment. This farmhouse, built in 1738, still stands on the side of Breakneck Hill. It is known locally in Middlebury as the Old Bronson Place. Titus Bronson was born in a house a half-mile away that stood until 1833.

The Old Bronson Place has been completely restored to reflect its colonial heritage and craftsmanship, thanks to the vision of hard work of Esther and Larry Duryee. In the summer of 1940 they bought the deteriorating house. As Mrs. Duryee wrote in an article for the *Old Home Journal:*

> *Each time we inspected this ramshackle house we saw unpainted brown shingles covering the sightly piles of hundred-year old manure, and a rickety barn at the bend in the road . . . somewhere behind this forbidding scene was a promise — a picture of colonial charm, lawns and intimate gardens, fields of well-cared for alfalfa — a vague dream which ultimately might come true. Standing there for two centuries against the wind, snow, and summer storms had not fundamentally changed the structure. All the Old Bronson Place needed was love . . . nobody who lived in this house ever had enough money to spoil it.[1]*

Visible from the front door of the Bronson house, is a portrait, in shades of brown, of Josiah Bronson at 80 years of age. Josiah was a younger brother to Titus Bronson's paternal grandfather, Isaac. The portrait is a reproduction of the original painting by William Jennys, which now hangs in the Mattatuck Museum in Waterbury, an industrial center adjacent to Middlebury. A few blocks from the museum are records containing the roots of Titus Bronson and the rest of his family at the Silas Bronson Library. Silas Bronson was born in the Old Bronson Place the same year his distant cousin Titus. Silas Bronson went on to become a prosperous New York City merchant. At his death he bequeathed the city of Waterbury $200,000 for the library.

The name Bronson was derived from the baptismal name Brownson — son of Brown. Once in the mid 18th century, three Bronson brothers signed the same document: Bronson, Brounson, and Brunson. John and Frances Brownson changed the spelling of their name to Brunson after they arrived in the New World on October 8, 1635, on a ship named "Defense." Along with them were their two daughters, John's brother Richard, and his sister Mary.

John and Frances Brownson participated in a mass exodus known in American history as the Great Migration. During the decade of the 1630's 45,000 men, women, and children pulled up their roots to cross the Atlantic Ocean in frail and cramped ships. The passage of 3,000 miles usually took about three months. In a sense, the Great Migration marked the beginning of the American Westward Movement. These English emigrants, most of them Puritans of varying degrees of commitment and intensity, were our first pioneers. They were the first dreamers of the American Dream, which they might have defined as a simple life of human decency in a local context, with a minimum of social hierarchy.

Many of us perceive these 17th century Puritans as pleasure-hating fundamentalists, gloomy kill-joys, narrow-minded, prudish, and moralistic people who lived, as H.L. Mencken once put it, under the "haunting fear that someone somewhere, may be happy." This stereotypical proposition has some basis in fact, although it ignores the complexity and positive side of Puritanism. The image of the Puritan preacher as the white-wigged prophet-in-black threatening hellfire upon all who slept in church or sold a dozen eggs on Sunday is misleading. The Puritan ministers generally did not play upon their congregations' nerves by depicting the horrors of eternal damnation in hell. Puritan preachers wanted their flocks' faith to rest on sound intellectual conviction.

The Puritans appreciated many of life's pleasures. They made love, liked strong drink, danced, sang, played games, wore colorful garments, and greatly respected the powers of logic and reason. The Puritans' social life was characterized by many festive days: election days, militia training days, town meeting days, and weddings. Even funerals became occasions for community gatherings to make merry, gossip, and eat. However, the truly committed Puritan always tried to be conscious of a higher purpose: the glorification of God. "Where do you stand with God today?" was a daily question of self-examination for the sincere Puritan. What distinguished the 17th century

Puritans was their attempt to integrate theology into everyday life; Puritanism was a noble experiment in applied theology.

During the late 1560's the term "Puritan" came into common usage. The Puritans received their name because they were English Protestants intent on "purifying" the Church of England of any lingering traces of Catholicism. In their eyes the Anglican Church was still tainted with popery and needed to be purified — made more strictly Protestant. A London congregation which met secretly at a place called Plumber's Hall described themselves as the "pure and stainless religion." Their contemporaries labeled them "Puritans or unspotted lambs of the Lord."

By the 1580's the Congregationalist conception of the convenanted church began its ferment among the Puritan ranks. The Puritan Movement developed a radical fringe. As soon as the idea of the convenanted church took hold in the minds of the zealots and fanatics, they were confronted with a logical deduction: if the true, "pure" church is founded on personal volition and not on geographical location, then they could no longer in good conscience remain within a national church. Their only recourse was to "separate" from their own church, an act equivalent in the legal system of the time to high treason. One group of Separatists fled to Holland and then to the New World. There, in 1620, they founded Plymouth Colony and became the "Pilgrims" of American history and legend.

By the 1630's, the decade of Great Migration, Puritanism had developed into a counterculture. In 1629, King Charles I of England dissolved Parliament, a move that did not improve his flagging popularity among a large portion of the British population. Charles' fiscal policies proved as unpopular as his politics. Royal taxation was not especially oppressive to any class of society; the problem was that the taxes were levied in an unconstitutional and arbitrary manner and were used for purposes which many taxpayers regarded as immoral.

One major Puritan demand was for a more dynamic preaching ministry. At the heart of Puritan unrest was the criticism of preaching in the Elizabethan Church. The Puritans were fed up with the "dumb dogs of the establishment" who read verbatim from the homilies prepared by their uninspired superiors. Richard Greeham, the patriarch of Puritan preachers, lamented that many ministers "preach and delight to hear plausible novelties, to please the ear, rather than the simple power of the word to pierce the heart . . . They take the bone and refuse the marrow."

In 17th century England the church and state were intimately linked. All citizens were members of the Church of England. They had to attend the local parish church under penalty of fine and were forced to listen to sermons preached by a parson whose personality and politics they disagreed with. Control of the pulpit was a political issue. King Charles I said "the dependency of the church upon the crown is the chiefest support of regal authority." Frequently ministers had to read government handouts and were told what positions to take on delicate political matters. In our time, the first action of a revolutionary group would be to take control of the broadcasting system. During the 17th century the Puritans' most important action was to take control of the church.

Eventually the momentum of the Puritan movement led to the English Revolution of the 1640's. This was a time when:

> . . . there was a great overturning, questioning, revaluing, of everything in England. Old institutions, old beliefs, old values came into question . . . There was a period of glorious flux and intellectual excitement . . . Literally everything seemed possible; not only were the values of the old hierarchical society called in question but also the new values, the Protestant Ethic itself . . . What was new in the 17th century was the idea that the world might be permanently turned upside down.[2]

The Puritan Revolution of the 1640's culminated in the trial of King Charles I, who was condemned as a "tyrant, traitor, murderer, and enemy of his country" and consequently executed one January morning in 1649. Much of Europe was aghast; The execution sent shivers of horror through every court in Europe. Kings had been killing one another for centuries; parricide, fratricide, and assassination were old and familiar events. But that a substantial part of a national population would rise up, try its king for disloyalty, mischief, and treachery, and then condemn and kill him was something new. Radical Puritans had gone beyond the ideas and conscience of their time. As H.G. Wells stated in *The Outline of History,* "It was as if a committee of jungle deers had taken and killed a tiger — a crime against nature."

Following the Puritan Revolution, was a period of restoration where the king, lords, court, bishops, and Anglicanism reappeared. "Milton's nation of prophets became a nation of shopkeepers." The radicalism of the Revolution lost much of its verve and appeal. In America, as historian Samuel Huntington has pointed out, radicalism

> spread and diffused to become the core of a credo for a new society; England had a Puritan Revolution without creating a Puritan society; America created a Puritan society without enduring a Puritan Revolution.[3]

The legacy of the Puritan Revolution is permanently lodged deep in the American consciousness. Huntington argues, with ample justification, that the Puritan Revolution was "the single most important formative event of American political history." The Puritan Revolution of the 1640's was the original source for the two dominant characteristics of American political history: the close intermingling of religion and politics, and the moral passion "that has powered the engines of political change in America." Huntington perceives the essence of Puritanism as intense moralism:

> The quintessential quality of a Puritan was not the acceptance of any given body of doctrine, but a driving enthusiasm for moral improvement in every aspect of life, 'a holy violence in the performing of all duties.'

The Puritans were America's prototype "cranky" true believers. The descendants of the Puritans, people like Titus Bronson, became known as Yankees. They passed on traits of the Puritan mind and personality in a variety of pursuits all the way across the continent. Many of these qualities — piety, sobriety, propriety, thrift, "steady habits," and "book learning" — have persisted into our time.

In June, 1630, the first large group of Puritan settlers, led by John Winthrop, arrived in the New World. They founded Boston, which would quickly become the nucleus of the Massachusetts Bay colony and the bridgehead from which more than 20,000 Puritan pioneers would enter the wilderness to Massachusetts, Vermont, Connecticut, Rhode Island, Maine, New Hampshire, and parts of eastern New York.

Three years later the greatest Puritan preacher of the 17th century, Thomas Hooker, arrived in Boston after a harrowing escape from England. Hooker and his party were assigned by the colony to New Town (now Cambridge). Life in New Town proved to be more complicated than Hooker and his friends had anticipated. Many strong personalities lived in this frontier community. Disagreements over religious and other issues developed. Hooker and his flock felt a restlessness and a "strong bent of their spirits to remove thither." They heard stories about the fertile Connecticut River Valley to the west. They petitioned the General Court for permisson to leave, citing the need for more land as their chief reason. The permission was granted. Eventually, in the spring of 1636, Hooker and his entire congregation of more than one hundred headed west to the beautiful wilderness of the Connecticut River Valley.

As Hooker's migratory congregation traveled "over mountains, through swamps and thickets," and across rivers "which were not passable save with great difficulty," they sang Psalms and made the woods ring with laughter. They were a happy and contented group who enjoyed walking, sleeping under the stars, and the general feeling of togetherness and adventure. They followed the old, narrow Indian trails, probably the Bay Path (roughly today's U.S. 20) westward and the Old Connecticut Path (which followed a route just south of the present I-86) southwesterly, passing near the present town of Woodstock, Mansfield, and Manchester until they reached the Connecticut River at Podunk (East Hartford). They settled near the Dutch fort with the other New Town pioneers.

Within a year more than 800 people populated the three river towns of Hartford, Wethersfield, and Windsor.

Bronson family genealogists suggest the likelihood that John Brownson was one of the company who came to Connecticut with Hooker in 1636. John Brownson was born in September, 1602, in the small village of Lamarsh in Essex County, England, the same county where Thomas Hooker preached before he left the country for Holland. It was a hotbed of Puritanism; chances are very good that John Brownson heard Hooker preach and was thus inspired to emigrate to the New World.

In 1639 John Brownson was mentioned on the list of Hartford settlers who, by the "town's courtesie," had liberty "to fetch woods and keep swines or cowes on the common." Brownson's house lot was in the "soldier's field" located in the north part of the old village of Hartford on the Neck Road. Brownson was probably granted land for his service in the Pequot War. Records of 1640 show that he and a neighbor, Andrew Warner, were fined five shillings "for putting their hogs over the Great River and five shillings for each day they left them there."

The role of a strong personality in the founding of new Connecticut towns, as exemplified by the leadership displayed by Thomas Hooker, typified the independent spirit that marked the early history of Connecticut. During the 17th century, Connecticut became one of the most insular and decentralized of the American colonies. This isolation was due to its geographic location. The citizens of Connecticut lived placid and peaceful lives. Generally, they submitted willingly to the authority of their preachers and magistrates. Connecticut came to be known as the Land of Steady Habits — a place of orthodox beliefs and traditional ways. Conformity became one of the most distinguishing features and characteristics of the emerging Connecticut Yankee, along with a certain restlessness. Restlessness began to manifest itself in 1640 when settlers from the river towns of Hartford, Wethersfield, and Windsor headed west beyond a small mountain range to found Farmington. These pioneers exhibited the fundamental urge so characteristic of the evolving Yankees — the desire to possess more land of their own. Possession of land, these neophyte Yankees believed, was the basis of their economic and political freedom.

John Brownson and his brother Richard helped found Farmington. Generally, second-generation towns like Farmington followed a method of land distribution derived from the original settlements and based on the common law procedures of England. When a town was incorporated, all the "freemen" — those who met the qualifications for voting in town elections — had a voice in the distribution of the land. The amount of land granted to a family compensated for the difference in quality or location. This system was known as "sizing." A local committee of "sizers" chose a piece of land typical of that to be divided. This served as a "pattern." If the particular parcel of land in question did not fit the "pattern" in fertility and distance from the town common, the "sizers" committee added land to the grant. This additional land was free from taxes. If the land was exceptionally located or more fertile than the pattern, the committee decreased the amount granted. So it was that everyone was assured reasonably fair treatment.

Usually a parcel of land in the center of the town was set aside as a common for all citizens to use. Here the church and/or meetinghouse was erected. Often the common was located at the crossroads or on either side of the main street. The meetinghouse became the focal point of the community in early Connecticut towns and was the most centrally located building. Rich and powerful town leaders built their homes near the common and meetinghouse, and it was used not only as a place of worship, but also as a town hall and public storehouse for military supplies. Nearby stood other public buildings and facilities such as the schoolhouse, the blacksmith shop, the general store, the inn, the jail, the whipping post, and pillory.

After studying the ancestry of Titus Bronson, genealogist Ethel W. Williams concluded that "the Bronsons possessed an inherent genius for selecting appropriate townsites."[5] John Brownson was one of the first settlers of Hartford, Connecticut and one of the founding fathers of Farmington. John's third child, Isaac Brownson (Titus Bronson's great-great grandfather) was part of a group of about 30 Farmington citizens who in 1674 purchased the site of present-day Waterbury, Connecticut from native American occupants. The Farmington pioneers called it the Plantation of Mattatuck, an Indian word meaning "badly wooded region." In 1686 Mattatuck was incorporated as a village and renamed Waterbury. Isaac Brownson "had a meadow allotment and was named in all the divisions of the common fence." Genealogist Williams tells us, "He appears to have complied promptly with all the conditions of the Articles of Settlement." Isaac was involved in the original organization of the Waterbury Congregational Church, and was a petitioner to the General Court of Connecticut for liberty "to gather" a church in Waterbury. He was one of its seven pillars at its final organization in 1691. At different times he was active on the school committee, was the town surveyor, and prominent in the local militia. His nickname was the "Sergeant." Williams surmises that Isaac "Sergeant" Brownson "seems to have been one of the most respected of the early settlers of Waterbury."

As the 17th century came to a close, population patterns changed dramatically throughout Connecticut. The land began to wear out and the quest was for new farm lands on both sides of the Connecticut River Valley. Before 1690 there were only thirty towns in Connecticut. By 1720 twenty new towns were settled.

In the late 1660's, Isaac Brownson married Mary Root, the daughter of John Root from Farmington. Isaac and Mary had nine children. Their first child, Isaac Brownson, Jr., born in 1670, was Titus Bronsons's great-grandfather. When he was 31 years old Isaac Jr. married Mary Morgan, the daughter of Richard Morgan, Sr., of New London. The same year (1701) Isaac Jr. purchased twelve acres from Thomas Warner on the south side of Woodbury Road, of Breakneck Hill. According to genealogist Williams, Isaac Jr. went to live on this land during March, 1707, and is considered the first permanent white settler on what is today Middlebury, Connecticut.

Isaac Jr. and Mary Bronson produced nine children. According to family records, their eldest son and second child, Isaac Bronson III, was the first white child born within the corporate limits of Middlebury. The historic date was March 27, 1707. Isaac III lived to be 93 years of age. He is buried in Middlebury Cemetery a few feet from his grandson Titus Bronson. Isaac's epitaph reads, "Here lieth interred the body of Mr. Issac Bronson, who departed this life Dec. 7th AD 1799 in the 93rd year of his age. He was the first child born in this place."

Isaac Bronson married twice. In 1734 at the age of 27 he married Eunice Richards. Together they had seven children. Eunice died after giving birth to the seventh child, a daughter named Seth. When he was 43 years old, Isaac married Abigail Brockett, the widow of Calem Munson of Wallingford. Abigail and Isaac had two children. Their first child, named Titus, was born on October 3, 1751. He was the father of Kalamazoo's founder, Titus Bronson, Jr.

On April 19, 1775, at Lexington Green in Concord, Massachusetts, the Revolutionary War began with a skirmish between American volunteer militiamen and British soldiers. Titus Bronson, Sr. was 25 years old when news of the war beginning reached Middlebury. Like thousands of other young Americans, Titus, Sr. enlisted in the Revolutionary Army and in 1781, he re-enlisted. During his first hitch in the army, he was married to Hannah Cook, the daughter of Moses Cook and Sarah Culver. Hannah Cook was born in 1755 in Waterbury, Connecticut. At the age of 24, on December 9, 1779, she gave birth to her first child — a son named Jarius.

Titus Bronson, Sr. and his wife Hannah went on to have seven more children: Horace (February 15, 1782), Augustus (June 24, 1784), Esther (October, 19, 1786), Titus, Jr. (November 27, 1788), Hannah (April 18, 1791), Sally (September 13, 1794), and Leonard (June 24, 1797).

The family was the basic social and religious unit. The Puritan family was generally an example of piety and filial respect. The authority of the father over his wife and children was absolute. Behind the figure of the father stood the powerful presence of the magistrates and the clergy. When a woman married, she surrendered everything to her husband. She fell under his complete authority and devoted herself exclusively to the management of the household. Large families were the rule, and an economic and social necessity. Several generations lived under the same roof. Daughters married at 16 or 17 and frequently had six or seven children in rapid succession and often died in childbirth.

The childrens lives were not easy. They were treated like small adults — little men or women dressed in the same clothing styles as their parents. At the dinner table they were forbidden to speak unless spoken to, and were expected to eat, without question, whatever was served them.

Servants were considered members of the household. In 17th century America, anyone who worked for another in any capacity was considered a servant, regardless of whether it was in a voluntary or involuntary capacity. Voluntary servants were hired, apprenticed, or indentured, usually for seven years. Involuntary servants were either black or Indian, but slaves were never held in any significant number in Connecticut.

Titus Bronson, Jr. was five months old when George Washington was inaugurated as the first president of the United States. The ceremony took place on the final day of April, 1789, on the second story, porticoed balcony of Manhattan's Federal Hall, which overlooked the rumbling traffic of Wall Street. New York City was, at the time, the new nation's temporary capital and its second largest city, with a population of approximately 35,000. The distinction of largest city in the country belonged to Philadelphia, having 42,000 residents. Detroit, which was founded in 1701, was basically a frontier fort. Chicago was a wilderness trading post, although by the time of Titus Bronson's death in 1853 it would boast a population of 30,000 people. The census of 1790, the first in American history, reported that only five percent of the American population could be classified as "urban," in which the term was defined as an incorporated village of 2,500 or more people. The vast majority of the population lived on farms within about 100 miles of the Atlantic Ocean. Many sections of the country had no real roads; what were depicted as roads on maps were often little more than bridle paths or blazed trails. Stagecoaches and heavy wagons could travel only on roads connecting major cities. The road between Philadelphia and New York was probably the most heavily traveled highway in America, with stages running daily. Two full days were required to cover the 100 miles. A few roads — like the Wilderness Road blazed by Daniel Boone through the Cumberland Gap in Kentucky — penetrated the mountain barriers to the west. As historian James MacGregor Burns has observed: "As Americans gained their liberty from Britain in the 1780's, they had only the most general idea of the great lands stretching to the west."

On December 29, 1790, when Titus Bronson, Jr. was a little over two years old, the Connecticut General Assembly granted "West Farms" and adjoining points of Southbury and Woodbury the privilege of becoming a separate ecclesiastical society by the name of Middlebury. The name Middlebury was derived from its position six miles from Waterbury, Southbury, and Woodbury.

Until 1760 most of the settlers of Middlebury were connected with the First Congregational Church in Waterbury. In 1757, thirty-five Middlebury families petitioned the General Assembly for "winter privileges:" the right to hold religious services at some central point in the winter months. This request was denied, but three years later, in 1760, another petition was submitted. This time the Assembly granted the petitioners' request and winter privileges were granted.

Middlebury's struggle for independence from Waterbury followed the typical pattern of most New England towns in the 17th and 18th centuries. As time went on, town after town in New England grew too large. Good farmland became scarce and the population was geographically scattered. Meetings were hard to attend, and reaching consensus on local issues such as the location of roads was difficult. Since towns then were also ecclesiastical societies or districts, often the "outlivers" would petition for winter privileges, or would seek permission to secede to found their own separate ecclesiastical societies and towns on the periphery of the old one — like bees hiving off for a new home. Houses were built farther and farther away from the central meetinghouse. When enough outlying residents became frustrated with the inconvenience of traveling so far to meetings or to attend to civic duties, they demanded recognition as a separate village with their own church, taxes, and elected officals.

The settlers living within the centers of crowded towns opposed the requests of their outlying neighbors for economic and political reasons, although these conflicts were expressed in religious terms. Taxes were levied to support a minister for the town church, to take care of roads, and to help the poor. If a portion of the village's population left, revenue would be lost. The citizens living near the center of town argued that the petitioners were poor people trying to avoid taxes; or radical separatists seeking a minister more sympathetic to their world view; or persons with "an intolerant obsession with 'independency.'"

Historian Kenneth Lockridge has written extensively on the Hiving Effect and agrees that many of these arguments made sense:

> The outlivers were often reacting to the increasing social hierarchy, formalistic established religion, and elitist policies of the old center of town by seeking to establish a new town exclusively occupied by people such as themselves.[6]

Many times these outlivers were subsistence farmers desiring a more unified religious experience along with a political leadership more connected with their interests. As one group of outlivers put it, "We desire to be free people of ourselves."

In 1800, the ecclesiastical society of Middlebury petitioned the Connecticut General Assembly for incorporation as a separate town. This petition was naturally opposed by many Waterbury residents who argued that they would lose some of their finest citizens.

On April 28, 1807, Middlebury tried again, arguing that there were 175 families within the limits of their ecclesiatical society; that Middlebury Center was six miles distant

from each of the towns of Waterbury, Watertown, Woodbury, Southbury, and Oxford; and that Middlebury was
separated from Waterbury by a rough and uninhabitable
tract of country.

In October of the same year the General Assembly
resolved "that the Ecclesiastical Society of Middlebury
shall be incorporated into a separate and distinct township
called Middlebury."

On November 16, 1807 — eleven days before Titus
Bronson Jr.'s nineteenth birthday — Middlebury held its
first town meeting in the Congregational Church which
had been erected fourteen years earlier on the village
green. Town officers were chosen and the long sought-
after independence was celebrated.

Notes

[1]Larry Duryee, "The Bronson Saga," *Old Home Journal* (Winter
1974).

[2]Samuel Huntington, *American Politics — The Promise of Dishar-
mony* (Cambridge: Harvard University Press, 1981), p. 153.

[3]ibid., p. 153.

[4]ibid., p. 153.

[5]Ethel W. Williams, "Ancestry of Titus Bronson," *Michigan Heritage,* p. 108.

[6]Kenneth Lockridge, *Settlement and Unsettlement in Early America*
(New York: Cambridge University Press, 1981), p. 42.

See Also:

Bronson Lineage
    1636-1917
    Harriet Bronson Sibley
    Dallas, Oregon 1917
Bronson (Bronson, Brunson) Families   Col. Herbert Bronson
Enderton
    1969
Bronson, Brownson, Brunson
    Elsie Howlett Tracy
    La Jolla, California
    August, 1973
The Bronson Genealogy
    Rev. Charles N. Sinnett
    Carthage, South Dakota

Titus Bronson's cabin. He is talking to a visitor on horseback. Courtesy, Kalamazoo Public Library.

CHAPTER FOUR:

Rendezvous on the Road

During the Depression years of the late 1930's, while on the road in America, historian Alistair Cooke packed orange crates in his car trunk which contained Federal Writers Project travel guides for the states he planned to travel through. These books — officially called the American Guide Series — are valuable items of Americana. They directed Cooke to hundreds of places along the road that few tourists had visited or even heard about. "America," Cooke wrote, "which had no guide books worth the name, suddenly has a library of the best."

Michigan — A Guide to the Wolverine State, published in 1941, is one of the American Guide Series, and contains a treasure trove of information about pre-World War II Michigan. Delightful details abound in the Kalamazoo section of the guide. The Kalamazoo Municipal Airport on Portage Road was called Lindbergh Field, bus fare was a nickel, for a quarter you could take a taxi to any point within the city limits — add fifteen cents and you could play eighteen holes of golf at the city courses. "The one 'skyscraper,' a fifteen story bank building," we are informed, "looks down on peddlers hawking celery and peanuts — a sight peculiar to Kalamazoo."

However, some of the information about Titus Bronson is inaccurate. He is credited with being Kalamazoo County's first white settler, but that distinction belongs to Basil

Harrison. Also, Bronson is described as "an outspoken man who loved his liquor, a taste not shared by temperance-advocating big-wigs." Bronson's drunkeness is given as the chief reason for changing the town's name from "Bronson" to "Kalamazoo." This passage is the chief source of the erroneous characterization of Titus Bronson as a drunk that is still prevalent in the minds of many Kalamazoo citizens.

In the forward to the Michigan guide, a New Deal administrator defended the "unsung historians" who researched and wrote these travel guides against charges they were "boondogglers and pencil leaners." He described the conditions under which these "unsung historians" had to work:

> In some cases, their tools for acquiring information were deplorable. They had stubs of pencils and cheap waste paper to make notes upon. They had no automobiles, no paid transportation, but in many instances — thinly clothed and with belts put in — they thumbed their way to their rendezvous with their source materials.

Following in the tradition of the unsung historians of the 1930's, in July, 1979, I thumbed my way to source materials about Titus Bronson in Ohio and Connecticut; I had plenty of pens, a couple of blank notebooks, a back-pack filled with warm clothes and $100 cash hidden in my money belt.

It took me six rides and less than a day to hitchhike from Kalamazoo to Akron, Ohio — the first stop on my itinerary. Since Titus Bronson lived off and on for seven or eight years in Tallmadge, a suburb of Akron, I hoped the downtown Akron Public Library might contain sources of information on Titus. Within half an hour after walking through the front door of the library, I learned one of the major reasons why the founder of Kalamazoo emigrated from his hometown in Connecticut to Tallmadge, Ohio. Titus Bronson participated in one of the most influential migrations America has ever known — the Yankee Exodus.

Richard Lingeman, in his narrative history, *Small Town America* asked, "The dream of founding a town — how to account for it?" He suggested one answer, "Perhaps it was bred into the Virgin Territory of the Reserve." The "Reserve" was a three million acre, 120 mile long tract bodering Lake Erie just west of Pennsylvania known as The Western Reserve of Connecticut, "New Connecticut," or The Connecticut Western Reserve.

By the end of the American Revolution, seven of the thirteen states, including Connecticut, claimed lands west of the Appalachian Mountains. Under pressure to ratify the Articles of the Confederation, most of the states relinquished their western claims to the Federal government. Connecticut followed suit in 1786 but because it was land-poor, Connecticut retained for development the Western Reserve in what is now the northeast corner of Ohio. The western extremity of the Reserve, called the Firelands, was set aside as compensation for Connecticut citizens whose towns had been burned by the British troops. Connecticut gave up political control of the Reserve in 1800. Three years later, when the Ohio Territory attained statehood, it included the Western Reserve.

In 1795, a private group of Hartford speculators who called themselves the Connecticut Land Company, purchased 2.5 million acres of the Reserve, which was later methodically surveyed and sold, mostly to New Englanders. In 1796, General Moses Cleaveland, representing the company, led the first surveying party into the area. He laid out the town that was to bear his name (later losing the first "a" due to the haphazard spelling of the time). As Lingeman tells us, Cleveland's "first act, good New Englander that he was, was to pace off the outline of a ten-acre public square among the trees. That ritual done, he ordered his men to lay out a town around the square."

When Cleaveland returned East from his expedition, a public relations campaign began in full force to promote the Western Reserve as a wonderful place to emigrate. Hyperbolic stories about corn fourteen feet tall, soil black as gunpowder, and fields that were stoneless were common. The exodus to Ohio, however, wasn't considered a good development by everyone in the East. Fear of both social and economic changes that might follow the loss of population inspired bitter attacks on the idea of heading west. This fear was certainly not unfounded; whole towns picked up and left their homeland for the unknowns of the

Western Reserve wilderness. Some of the attacks upon Ohio fever were cutting, but amusing. Favorites of the Yankee press were cartoons depicting emigrants to Ohio in fine wagons drawn by sleek and fat horses, carrying robust men with smiling families. The next scene showed such people returning to New England after their Ohio fever had subsided, in wrecks of wagons with the sign "I have been to Ohio" attached to the side; the wagons now carried haggard, gaunt, and ragged passengers.

One Connecticut Yankee who emigrated to Ohio was a hot-eyed visionary and former missionary named David Bacon. In 1807 Bacon made a deal with Benjamin Tallmadge and Ephraim Starr whereby he would handle the land sales and surveying for Tallmadge township — land they had acquired in a drawing of the Connecticut Land Company. Bacon was one of the first missionaries of the Northwest to preach among Native Americans and was a former schoolteacher who taught at the frontier settlement of Detroit. For years he had dreamed of founding a religious community based on Puritan principles in the wilderness of the Connecticut Western Reserve. In 1807, he built a cabin on the site of present-day Tallmadge.

Richard Lingeman has observed that

> only the towns founded by religious groups seemed to have any semblance of a unifying vision in their layouts — any sense of community purpose or aspiration over and beyond the mundane practicalities of the real estate transaction.[1]

He offered Tallmadge, "a new England town run riot," as an example. David Bacon followed the New England model of the meetinghouse and a town hall on the village green at the center and roads leading to it. Instead of surveying the town into small salable lots, Bacon had the township divided into sixteen great lots of 1,000 acres each. Along the borders of these lots, running in each of the four directions, were roads 66 feet wide. Bacon had previously studied the original plan of Washington, D.C. and was influenced by it. He laid out roads radiating from each corner of the village green to the farthest corner of the township, and four other roads running in each of the directions. Double rows of elms were planted along these routes. As Lingeman asserts, "The results were aesthetically pleasing as well as theologically sound."

Initially, Bacon had little difficulty attracting settlers to his settlement. They came from Connecticut and other New England States. However, the initial harmony based on a shared religious vision soon deteriorated. Historian Harlan Hatcher points out that Bacon and his followers

> *lived by a rigorous Puritan moral code. But no man has yet devised a scheme to hold permanently together a group of human families under a single code. Money and minor points of doctrine, together with clashes of personality, always shatters the brotherhood.*[2]

Bacon's sophisticated road system — which was ahead of its time and more advanced than most piecemeal county systems — was not a cheap dream to maintain. A tax of two dollars was levied per 100 acres "to be paid for the support of the gospel," which meant among other items, the road system. This tax was objected to vigorously by many land buyers who took the issue to court. The tax was ruled illegal. This reversal of fortune undermined the financial foundation of Bacon's religious community. Bacon could not meet his mortgage payments and consequently went bankrupt. He left Tallmadge in 1812.

After the War of 1812 the momentum of the Yankee Exodus picked up steam. A decade earlier, Lewis and Clark had made their famous trek across the continent. Their journals, published in 1814, fired the imaginations of many restless and discontented Yankees in New England. Between 1815 and 1850, growth in America in all directions proceeded in wave after wave. In that single generation the nation's territory almost doubled, sweeping from the Mississippi Valley to the Pacific Ocean. The population tripled and the national wealth increased five-fold. Science and technology advanced along with education, agriculture, and industry.

The people in the forefront of this growth and change were the Yankees of New England. The Yankees possessed energy, vision, industry, and earnestness. These traits combined with a strong urge to see, with their own eyes, if the grass on the other side of the mountain was really greener, produced a restlessness characteristically American. For some, however, the grass would never be quite the right shade; families often moved four of five times in a single generation.

"I remember well the tide of emigration through Connecticut, on its way to the West during the summer of 1817," wrote Samuel Goodrich. The summer of 1817 was known as "1800 and froze to death." Severe frosts occurred every month of the year. Goodrich continued:

> Thousands feared or felt that New England was destined, henceforth, to become a part of the frigid zone . . . A sort of stampede took place from cold, desolate, worn-out New England . . . Some persons went in covered wagons — frequently a family consisting of father, mother, and nine small children, with one at the breast — some on foot, and some crowded together under the cover, with kettles, gridirons, feather-beds, crockery, and the Family Bible, Watt's Psalms and Hymns, and Webster's Spelling book . . . Others started in ox-carts, and trudged on at the rate of ten miles a day. In several instances I saw families on foot — the father and boys taking turns in dragging an improvised hand-wagon, loaded with the wreck of household goods — occasionally giving the mother and babe a ride. Many of these persons were in a state of poverty, and begged their way as they went.[3]

By the early 1800's the population of Connecticut was over a quarter of a million people, although almost three times that number had migrated. As Yankee historian W. Storrs Lee put it, "For every individual who remained, three had gone over the hill. In many a town, people moved away faster then others moved in."

In Titus Bronson's hometown of Middlebury, Connecticut, there were many people feeling the itch to take off and head west to the Reserve, including Jarius and Augustus Bronson, two of Titus Bronsons' brothers. In January, 1819, Jarius, Augustus, and a fellow townsman, Ebeneezer Richardson, set forth on an exploratory trip to "look the land" of "New Connecticut." Jarius had been farming 25 acres on

Breakneck Hill and was finding it difficult to eke out a living for his family. Often in American history a common reason given for emigration was lack of good farmland. Sometimes this reason was valid, and sometimes the quest for better land was a disguise for restlessness, wanderlust, and a reluctance to engage in less extravagant exploitation of the soil. Jarius sold his farm and headed west to the Reserve with his brother and neighbor. They arrived in Tallmadge in March, 1817, purchased adjoining lots from Benjamin Tallmadge, and immediately planted corn and oats. On Augustus' lot they constructed a small cabin. In June they returned East for their families and to outfit themselves for the final trip back to Tallmadge.

On August 25, 1819, the families of Jarius and Augustus Bronson bade farewll to other family members and friends. In early September they visited relatives in Otsego and Oneida counties in New York state. In Augusta, New York, they were stricken with dysenterry and two of the children died. They arrived in Buffalo, New York distraught and discouraged. Among other things, they were concerned about the lateness of the season and feared that inclement weather might prevent them from completing their journey to Tallmadge. Lying in Buffalo Creek was an idle schooner with a captain seeking cargo to transport. At the captain's suggestion Jarius and Augustus decided to ship their supplies and equipment on this vessel. Relinquishing the last of their money, they loaded on board all of their possessions, except necessities they needed for the overland trip. With light wagons they soon arrived in Cleveland only to learn that the crew of the schooner had divided the ship's cargo and fled. Finally, on October 23, 1819, in a nearly destitute condition, they arrived in Tallmadge. The two families lived in Augustus' cabin until Jarius could build his own. About five weeks later, Jarius, his wife Irene and their children moved into their own crude quarters.

Upon arriving in Tallmadge, Jarius' 15 year old son Charles helped clear the land and plant crops. Charles lived on the farm until the day he died — April 11, 1896. One county historian called Charles "one of the most reliable and painstaking local historians of Summit County." Charles put together what is known today as *The Bronson Book,* a copy of which is in the local history area of the Akron Public Library. This book was originally written on strong heavy paper and bound in tough leather. It contains accounts of the early settlement of the Connecticut Western Reserve. Charles Bronson interviewed many pioneers and publishes some of the accounts in his book. He tells a story about his parents; they had just moved into their cabin and had no furniture, causing embarrassment to Irene, his mother. They used logs to sit on. At one point, in exasperation, Irene asked her husband, "What if the parson calls, I can't ask him to have a chair?" Jarius pondered the question for a few seconds and replied, "Just tell him to be seated."

On Christmas Eve, 1821, many of Tallmadge's citizens took part in beginning construction of the town church. For hours people dragged logs from the woods which were to be sawed into lumber for the church. It took almost four years to complete the church, but the final product was certainly worth the wait and hard work. The shingles were hewn from a single chestnut tree. The four stately white columns at the front of the church were shaped from solid walnut logs. On September 8, 1825, the Tallmadge Congregational Church was officially dedicated. Today it is considered an excellent example of the pure Connecticut-type of Federal architecture. It is the oldest church in Ohio to be continually used as a place of worship. A photograph of the church is on the cover of the 1944 Thanksgiving issue of *Life* magazine.

Chances are that Titus Bronson helped build Tallmadge's famed New England style church. Nineteenth century historian A.D.P. Van Buren tells us in his biographical sketch of Titus Bronson that it was in 1821 or 1822 that "we first hear of him pitching his tent at Tallmadge, Ohio."

It took me about a day to hitchhike the 400 miles between Tallmadge and Middlebury, Connecticut a "bedroom community" of almost 4,000 people. There is no formal downtown, but instead a charming and classic New England village green highlighted by the town hall and a Congregational Church built in the 1840's.

In the town hall, using Middlebury's "vital records," I discovered a piece of paper about the size of a check. Written across it in brown ink was the following: "Middlebury, Jan. 18, 1827. This may certify that Titus Bronson of Anarbor [sic] Michigan and Mrs. Sally Bartholomew of Tallmadge, Ohio have this day been united in marriage. Mark Mead, minister of the gospel."

During my week's stay in Middlebury, I took a bus to Hartford, the capital of Connecticut, which is about fifty miles northeast of Middlebury. In the Connecticut State Library' I made two significant discoveries. The first was a file containing a January 6, 1953 *Kalamazoo Gazette* article about Titus Bronson, along with a letter, also written in January, 1953, from a Kalamazoo resident, Jane S. Hagle. In her letter to the library she related numerous facts about Titus Bronson. She wrote:

> *I doubt if anyone has ever tried to put together the story of his life here and the influence on the place. It should be written up by someone with an understanding heart and a snoopy nose . . . Titus Bronsons's story is one of injustice, poverty, and heartache. I wish that more Kalamazoo people understood how badly treated he was so long ago.*

I learned after my return to Kalamazoo that Jane Hagle was a resident at a local nursing home. I interviewed Mrs. Hagle and she had a major influence on my thoughts regarding Titus Bronson. For years she had researched his life and had developed an intense empathy for him. She believed Titus Bronson was a very affectionate father and that his two daughters, Eliza and Julia, were godsends to him. She also emphasized how the relocation of the federal land office to Bronson village in 1834 affected the Bronsons. She pointed out that Titus Bronson was lame and in pain most of his life, and that the strangers who arrived in Bronson after the land office was relocated there had a lot of time on their hands and therefore looked around for ways to amuse themselves. She conjectured that many of them probably ridiculed Titus Bronson for the funny way he walked and talked. She reasoned that ultimately these abusive strangers made life for Titus and Sally Bronson unbearable and eventually caused them to leave the town they had founded. Jane Hagle also helped me understand Sally Bronson and how difficult it must have been for her to leave her home and friends to head west once again with her eccentric husband.

My other discovery in the Connecticut State Library was a book entitled *The Yankee Exodus,* written by Stewart Holbrook and published in 1950. I randomly opened the book to this paragraph:

> *For reasons long since lost in the mists, Kalam-zaoo County turned out to be the goal of many Vermonters. Cyrus Lovell left Grafton in 1829 to build the first frame house in Kalamazoo City; other Lovells named Enos, George W., and Lafayette W. were among the first settlers in nearby Climax. The first white child born in the country was William Rufus Shafter, the son of Hugh and Eliza, who had migrated from Windsor, Vermont ... A leading spirit in the founding of Kalamazoo College was Nathaniel Balch, from Athens, Vermont. Early Yankees in neighboring Schoolcraft village were Edwin H. and George Van Ness Lothrop from Boston, Massachusetts.[4]*

This paragraph appeared in a chapter entitled "The Land of Michigandia." Holbrook had speculated on the same question I had posed about Titus Bronson: Why would someone leave a familiar place for a frontier largely unknown except to trappers? Holbrook wrote in an ironic tone that "if it wasn't the weather, or the plague, or mortgage, or the restlessness conjured up by revivals it could be a pregnant maid on a hilltop farm."

The discovery of Holbrook's book was a turning point in my quest for the historical Titus Bronson. I began seeing the founder of Kalamazoo as a part of the long and noble tradition of the Yankee people. I began to understand that the much-maligned Yankee race had a lot to do with molding the American character. As Holbrook points out, "Much of the energy and even more of the intellect which had characterized America stemmed from New England sources."

Two examples of the Yankee spirit in thought and action were Concord writers Ralph Waldo Emerson and Henry

David Thoreau. After I discovered Holbrook's *Yankee Exodus* I began to see Emerson and Thoreau's transcendentalism in the context of American history. I realized they were contemporaries of Titus Bronson, Andrew Jackson, and Daniel Boone. While Thoreau hoed his beans at Walden Pond and Emerson prepared lectures in his Concord study, pioneers like Titus Bronson were founding towns on the frontier of Jacksonian America. The west, the frontier — these were the dominant sources of national energy and vision during the nineteenth century. The possiblilities offered by the frontier provided plausibility to the grandiose generalizations of transcendental thought. Both the Westward Movement and the Transcendental Movement were powered by an optimism denying limitations, an optimism based on faith in the individual and the concept of self-reliance. The spirit of the frontier and the spirit of transcendentalism were different spokes of the same wheel. This spirit hinged on a sense of something beyond, of the open road and unlimited possibilty. Inherent in both movements were toughness and resiliency, a resolution to carry on as long as need be, and a passion to create values where none had existed before, be they spiritual values or the values of brick and mortar. The joy and satisfaction of creating a reality after the pattern of individual dreams sums up the essence of the frontier ethic, transcendental thought, and the American Dream.

Stewart Holbrook makes the point that it was inevitable that the Yankee race should be swallowed up by later immigrations and dissipated by the scattering of the Yankees themselves. However, there was, he argued, a residue of New England character in all parts of our land strong enough to impress itself in some measure upon non-Yankees who in their second generations are less like their European ancestors than they are like the people who once lived in Plymouth and around the shores of Massachusetts Bay.

Titus Bronson's signature as Justice of the Peace. Courtesy, Western Michigan University Archives.

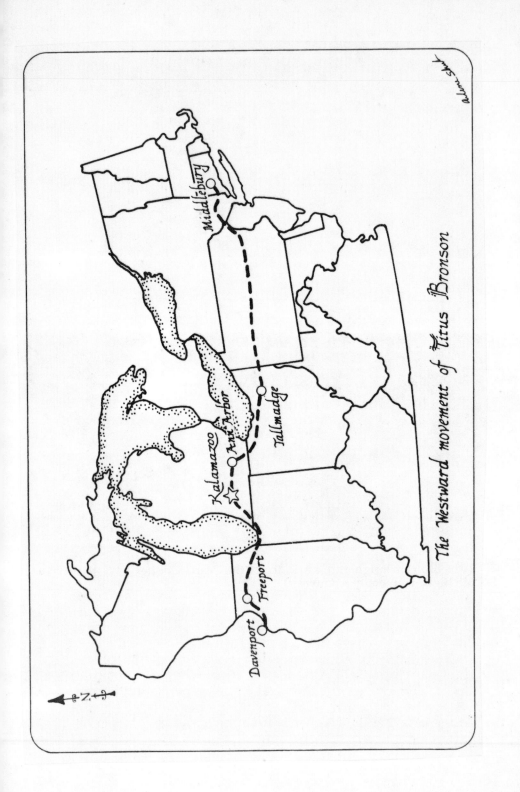

The Westward movement of Titus Bronson

CHAPTER FIVE:
Too Thick, Too Thick

> *Titus Bronson was a natural frontiersman. He belonged to the advanced Leatherstocking grade of civilization, and loved the ways of frontier life better than town life . . . He liked life in the new settlement, up to the time the speculator, the drone, the cheat, the scamp, and the politician came in, and then he thought it was time for him to go into the woods again, to get rid of these pests.*
>
> *—Historian A.D.P. Van Buren*

One day in 1835 or early 1836 Titus Bronson was taking a walk along a street in the frontier settlement he had founded when an acquaintance of his, Jesse Earl of Galesburg, approached him with the question, "How are you, Mr. Bronson?"

"Pretty well, pretty well," Bronson responded, "But it's getting too thickly settled here for me — too thick, too thick — too many men around." After taking off his coat Bronson continued, "I can't stand it; I shall have to go further west, where there is more room."

Titus Bronson's answer is an example of one of the dominant themes in American folklore, the "elbow room" motif. This was given classic expression by Daniel Boone, who, when asked in 1789, at the age of 65, why he was leaving his beloved Kentucky for the frontier of Missouri, responded, "Too many people. Too crowded. Too crowded. I want more elbow room."[1]

When Titus Bronson spoke about Bronson village being "too thick" with people, the village was a boom town doing millions of dollars of land office business. Between the years 1834, when the Federal land office was moved from White Pigeon to Bronson, and 1837, the greatest land sales in American history took place. Most of the territories of Michigan, Wisconsin, and parts of Alabama, Mississippi, Louisiana, and Arkansas were sold during these years. Often labeled as "flush times," there was an abundance of money in circulation, making it "flush in every pocket." During the era the term "doing a land office business" originated. When Titus Bronson departed Kalamazoo there were over 60 Federal land offices, including three in the Michigan Territory. These were in Monroe, Detroit, and Kalamazoo. During this period in American history, there was no stock market as we know it today. Unimproved land and town lots were the major means of speculation. Michigan, in particular, was the path of a speculative hurricane during this era of flush times and land fever. Twenty-five million dollars were paid into the Federal Treasury in 1836, and five million came from land sales in Michigan. "Michigan Fever" had taken hold, infecting thousands of people in the East. Detroit was the main point of entry for the immigrants. As many as 2,000 people arrived in a single day on steamships and sailing vessels.

In 1836, the Kalamazoo land office sold more acres than any other land office in the history of the United States. Over 1.6 million acres were disposed of, accounting for over two million dollars in receipts. Since the problems of managing a land office rose in proportion to sales, the year 1836 presented some severe problems for the Kalamazoo land office staff. With the coming of spring, land-hungry men started forming lines outside the land office in the dark, to be near the doors when they opened with the rising sun. As the spring months wore on, lines outside the land office lengthened. Tempers frayed, voices became strident, and more whiskey was consumed. Inside the land office, paper work accumulated as clerks worked twelve hour days trying to keep up. In June the local newspaper, the *Michigan Statesman,* reported that during the previous month the local land office took in a half million dollars. "This is selling government land," the paper commented, "with a vengeance, and a parallel case to it we believe, cannot be shown." The *Detroit Democratic Free Press* commented on the land fever gripping the small community to the west:

> *We are informed that the village of Kalamazoo is literally thronged with purchasers. The public and private houses are full and . . . in some instances, they are compelled to retire to the barns for accommodations in the way of lodging.*

Finally, in June, 1836, the register of the land office, Abraham Edwards, closed the office doors for a couple weeks so he and his staff could regroup and catch their breath. The *Michigan Statesman* commented that the staff's "extraordinary exertions . . . to get through the applications on file before stopping sales have, indeed, fagged out all in the office; and driven two of the Register's clerks to their beds." T.S. Atlee, one of Register Abraham Edwards' clerks, liked to tell this story about his boss:

> *The old Major, at one time during a 'great land rush,' to save his picket fence and other property, from utter destruction, bought a load of shingles for the express use and benefit of the crowd, and had proclamation made, that every man might help himself, gratis, and whittle away to his heart's content. After that, every other person you passed between this and the Receiver's on both sides of the road, at the taverns, on the corners, and everywhere else, had a knife and shingle in hand and was cutting away for dear life. Any 'knowing one" could tell, by the way a man whittled, what progress he was making in a trade.*
> 2

The relocation of the federal land office to Bronson village marked a turning point in the growth of the settlement. Hundreds of land-hungry pioneers and speculators headed for Bronson, and many of them bought land in and around the town. The land office offered property for sale not only in Kalamazoo County, but also in Berrien, Cass, St. Joseph, Branch, Calhoun, Allegan, and Van Buren Counties. Almost three million acres of land were available for purchase through the office, which stayed open until 1859.

Until 1834 Schoolcraft village — located south of Bronson in the center of Prairie Ronde and layed out by Lucius Lyon in 1831 — was more prosperous then the settlement founded by Titus Bronson. However, after the removal of the federal land office to Bronson, along with a newspaper and bank, the competition for the most prosperous town in the county took a new direction. As one early Schoolcraft resident commented, "trade was more than ever diverted to Kalamazoo, and the village [Schoolcraft] wore that dilapidated and unthrifty appearance which always attends a state of stagnation in business."

Ultimately, what turned things around for Bronson village were the people who followed the land office. Two of the most prominent new arrivals were Epaphroditus Ransom and Thomas C. Sheldon.

Epaphroditus Ransom is the only Kalamazooan ever to be elected governor and the first state chief executive to be inaugurated in the new capital at Lansing. He arrived in Bronson with his family in the late fall of 1834. After spending a couple of weeks with some friends on Grand Prairie they moved into Titus and Sally Bronsons first log house on the corner of Church and Water Street. The Bronsons had built themselves a two-story frame home on what is today the site of St. Lukes Episcopal church on Lovell Street. The next year Ransom erected a house on what is now Burdick Street between the State Theater and the Kalamazoo Gazette. This residence was considered one of the best in southwestern Michigan. The home was torn down in 1961 and a section of the huge beams with their interlocking joints is in the Kalamazoo Public Museum.

Another prominent new arrival in 1834 was Thomas C. Sheldon, who was the receiver (treasurer) of the White Pigeon land office and continued in that capacity in Bronson. Sheldon already owned land in Bronson village and was one of its proprietors, along with Justus Burdick, Lucius Lyon, and Titus Bronson. Sheldon, Burdick, and

Lyon were good friends, supporters of the Democratic Party, and business partners in various ventures. They owned the Kalamazoo House together and in 1836 they formed a transportation company with some other Bronson village residents. The company built a large flagboat to transport cargo on the Kalamazoo River. One successful trip was made, but on a second voyage the craft, venturing on the treacherous waters of Lake Michigan, was wrecked between the mouths of Kalamazoo River and North Black River.

During the winter of 1835 and 1836 "a movement was set on foot," as historian Samuel Durant put it, to change the name of Bronson village and the township of Arcadia to Kalamazoo. The main movers behind plans to change the name were Thomas C. Sheldon, Lucius Lyon, and Justus Burdick. Lyon used his political influence with the state legislature to gain the name change. In a March 27, 1836 letter to Cyren Burdick, Lyon wrote "I shall attend to having the name of Bronson post office changed to Kalamazoo."

On April 2, 1836, the following act was passed:

> Be it enacted by the Senate and House of Representatives of the State of Michigan, that from and after the thirty-first day of March, instant, the name of the township of Arcadia, in the county of Kalamazoo, shall be changed and altered to that of Kalamazoo; and also the name of the village of Bronson shall be changed and hereafter known and called Kalamazoo, any law to the contrary notwithstanding.[4]

A week later the local weekly newspaper, the *Michigan Statesman,* commented that:

> By recent act of our legislature, the name of our village has been altered from Bronson to Kalamazoo. This is as it should be — our county, town-

*ship, and village have now the same name . . . the
word is euphonous and significant, and we think
in this, as in most cases, the Indian name should
be retained.*

Although one factor behind the name change was that
Kalamazoo sounded better than Bronson, and didn't pro-
voke associations with the settlement's eccentric founder,
there was another more prosaic reason behind the change.
A year before Titus Bronson arrived in Kalamazoo County
in the summer of 1829, a man named Jabez Bronson (no
relation to Titus) became the first white settler of Branch
County when he built a log cabin on a prairie that was
subsequently called Bronson Prairie. The post office in
Titus Bronson's settlement was "Bronson," while Jabez
Bronson's post office was "Bronson Prairie." Frequently
the two settlements were confused by people back east
sending mail, causing much inconvenience to the residents of Bronson village. Dr. Foster Pratt, a postmaster of
Kalamazoo during the 1860's, asserted that this was the
primary reason for changing the village's name:

> *The change from 'Bronson" to 'Kalamazoo' is
> by many supposed to be mainly due to the good
> taste of our early settlers. It is no gracious office to
> dispel this complimentary fancy; but the stern
> duty of the voracious historian compels us to say,
> that the record in the post office department at
> Washington discloses the fact, that our primitive
> Bronsonites were actuated mainly by a different
> motive. While the post office here was "Bronson,"
> there was one in Branch County, a P.O. called
> 'Bronson Prairie.' Now, the benighted people
> toward the sunrise [the East], ignorant, grossly
> ignorant of western geography, confounded
> these two offices in directing their letters, much
> to the chagrin and inconvenience of the Bronson-
> ites.*
>
> *The problem was solved by our city taking on its
> present melodious name and Bronson Prairie
> lopping off the Prairie.⁵*

The reason commonly given for Titus Bronson's depar-
ture in 1836 is that he was distressed by the name change.

There is some basis for this conclusion. As Frederick Curtenius pointed out, Titus Bronson possessed "an insatiable desire to identify his name with some giant achievement." However, reasoning that Titus Bronson left because his feelings were hurt is an oversimplification. He planned on leaving Kalamazoo months before the name change occurred. John Geddes, a friend of Bronson's from his Ann Arbor days, remembered Titus Bronson in a letter as a tall, raw-boned person of slovenly appearance, but a good judge of wild land: "The last I saw of Bronson was in the fall of 1835; he then told me he was intending to cross the Mississippi River and invited me to go along."

Titus Bronson had witnessed a phenomenal growth of the place he came to in 1829. In a mere seven years the settlement had grown into a village of almost a thousand people. In the article applauding the name change, the *Michigan Statesman* asserted "that no town in Michigan has outstripped [Kalamazoo] in the march of improvement." The paper, "for satisfaction of friends abroad" offered a statistacal summary of the village and its facilities in 1836:

> — *sixty frame dwellings, many of them large and well-finished.*
> — *three large "public houses."*
> — *six stores providing a variety of products from shoes and groceries to drugs and liquor.*
> — *thirty to forty carpenters and "house-joiners."*
> — *four brick and stone masons.*
> — *three cabinet makers.*
> — *four blacksmiths.*
> — *four tailors.*
> — *two saddle and harness makers.*
> — *one gold and silversmith.*
> — *one tanner and currier.*
> — *two clergymen.*
> — *six lawyers.*
> — *three doctors.*
> — *five saw and grist mills.*

Not only had Titus Bronson witnessed the phenomenal growth of Bronson village, he also saw Michigan mature into a separate state. When Bronson arrived in the Michigan Territory in 1821, the previous years federal census had listed 8,765 persons. By 1834 over 85,000 people populated the state. However much of the "land fever" activity of the mid-1830s was generated by speculators, not by pioneers who intended to make the territory their permanent home. Not all of these speculators were immoral "pests," as Titus Bronson called them. One example was John M. Gordon, a rising young banker and lawyer of moderate wealth from Baltimore. After carefully researching all possible alternatives for buying government land, Gordon concluded that Michigan land was a good investment. He was told that no one who bought public land at $1.25 an acre "is known ever to have lost any thing by a purchase and sale of real estate, nor are any sales of land made at second hand under $2.50 per acre." In the late summer and early fall of 1836, while Titus Bronson was heading further west, Gordon traveled across Southern Michigan. He used Bronson village as a base and made many on-the-spot examinations of land nearby. He ended up buying over 6700 acres of land, mostly in Berrien and Van Buren counties. He eventually sold the land for a good profit. During his travels Gordon kept a detailed journal. In the following entry he discusses the advantages of Bronson village.

The site [Bronson] was taken up a few years since at $1¼ per acre and this price would seem like wild speculation. The point however is an important one, on the head of boat navigation of the Kalamazoo. It is the land office, central in its position, and the county seat of a very rich & thriving county where population has some thousand souls added to it annually. If one considers that Mich. has none or few towns, that its population is pouring in at the rate of 50 thousand a year, that they have been accustomed to and must have their villages, that the soil of excellent quality generally, it will be perceived that these town speculations have a real basis of intrinsic value & are not like investment in town plats in old states, where the wants of the people have been supplied in this particular gradually with

their slow growth. Suppose New York without
towns & villages tomorrow, that all are sunk by an
earth quake. The wants of the people would soon
build them up again with great rapidity — such,
on a smaller scale, is the process in town manufac-
ture now going on in Mich.[6]

The history of Titus Bronson and his family after they left Kalamazoo is vague. In 1837 they were operating a hotel in Freeport, Illinois, which is today a town of 50,000, 150 miles northwest of Chicago. It is known that both of the Bronson daughters, Eliza and Julia, married men they met in Illinois. Eliza, the elder, married A.C. Hooker. Julia married Matthew Hanna in Green River, Illinois. In the 1840's Titus and his wife settled in what is today Betten-dorph, a suburb of Davenport, Iowa. According to histori-an A.D.P. Van Buren, the Bronsons owned a "magnificent farm" just above Davenport and opposite the upper end of Rock Island, Illinois. "Had he retained his land," Van Buren conjectured, "Bronson would have become a mil-lionaire:"

But trusting to the honesty of men who turned out
to be sharpers, he was swindled out of his title,
and thus deprived of great wealth. His wife dying
about this time, 1842, he was thrown penniless
upon his children for support. Removing to Hen-
ry County, Illinois, he lived for some years with
his daughter, Mrs. Hooker.

In the fall of 1852 Titus Bronson went back to his hometown of Middlebury, Connecticut, where he was taken sick at his brother Leonard's home. According to Van Buren, Titus Bronson

was ready to die as he had nothing more to live
for. He thanked God that after all his wanderings
his dying bed would be smoothed by the kind-
ness of his early friends and his dust be mingled

*with that of his father's. After a week's sickness he
died January 6, 1853.*

Titus Bronson was 64 years old at the time of his death.

Notes

[1]B.A. Botkin, *A Treasury of American Folklore* (New York: Bantan Books 1980) p. 155.

[2]T.S. Atlee, "Kalamazoo in 1835 and 1855," *Quarter Centennial Celebration of the Settlement of Kalamazoo, Michigan* (Kalamazoo Gazette Print, 1855) p. 51.

[4]Samuel Durant, *History of Kalamazoo, County, Michigan* (Philadelphia: Everts and Abbott, 1880) p. 220.

[5]1867-68 Kalamazoo City Directory.

[6]John Gordon, *Michigan History,* XLIII (1959) 448-49

EPILOGUE

. . . they [Americans] do and will remove as their avidity and restlessness incite them. They acquire no attachment to the Place: But wandering about seems engrafted in their Nature: and it is a weakness incident to it, that they Should forever imagine the Lands further off are still better than those which they are already settled.[1]

—John Murray, the Earl of Dunsmore and last British governor of Virginia, in a 1771 letter to his superiors in London

On Friday morning, February 25, 1984, I attended a service at Stetson Chapel on the campus of Kalamazoo College. The purpose of the service was to honor the life and memory of Titus Bronson. The chapel was being prepared to receive eight English change-ringing bells that were custom-cast at London's historic Whitechapel Bell Foundry (which fashioned the Liberty Bell in 1752). Each bell was named for a prominent nineteenth century person important in the history of Kalamazoo and was inscribed with a short quote from scripture. The inscription of the bell dedicated to Titus Bronson read, "Every valley shall be exalted." (Isaiah 40: 3).

Attending this service was a very special experience for me because in a way it marked the closing of my quest for the historical Titus Bronson which I had begun almost six years before. As I sat in the chapel along with 150 other people, I felt proud to be an American because I was proud of Titus Bronson.

I also felt anxiety and apprehension over what would be said about Titus Bronson. I felt protective of his history and reputation. Professor Waldemar Schmeichel delivered a sermon entitled, "You are the Darnedest Man I Ever Saw." Professor Schmeichel told the story of Titus Bronson and the founding of Kalamazoo. The professor's sermon demonstrated a unique understanding of the complex nature of Kalamazoo's founder. He recognized that Titus Bronson was a tragic hero, possessing a tragic flaw — an error he kept committing over and over again, causing suffering. Titus Bronsons's tragic flaw that undermined his life was a chronic restlessness that has become a definitive characteristic of Americans. Professor Schmeichel offered three perspectives on the life and work of Titus Bronson: Titus the city planner, Titus the moralist, and Titus the individualist. He then offered a fourth perspective summarizing the founder's life toward a tenatative unity — Titus the "beginner of things":

Let me offer this concluding perspective on Titus Bronson. To call him eccentric, a frontiersman, an individualist would, of course, capture significant elements of his personality and life. What impresses me as a consistent pattern for him, however, is the fact that Titus was good at beginnings, but he seems never to have learned to stay with something and to see it through to maturity. It seems that Bronson heard a warning that the task to which he had given himself was beginning to outgrow him. For to be able to go beyond beginnings one realizes how that which one has begun changes and needs to change. And with this changing task, I myself became a changing and changed person. The growth of the town he had founded challenged him to grow with it. Titus, however, refused that challenge and instead took "the town" to court again and again about issues of maturity. He lost the first time and again by appeal, and he discovered that the two Bronsons, the man and the town, were refusing each other. The first Bronson chose to remain a man of beginnings, the frontiersman of infancy settlement. The town Bronson chose to become Kalamazoo and with it an identity away from the simplicity and romanticism of the beginning to the involved interaction of social life.[2]

Nick Kekic came to Kalamazoo in 1970. He is a freelance writer with a Bachelor's Degree in English from Western Michigan University. Nick, a certified Elementary school teacher, began studying Titus Bronson in 1978. Photograph, Linda Newbury.